Praise for "Thirteen Moons"

Thirteen Moons is a significant book—a meticulous and detailed investigation into the place of the lunar calendar in the Northern Tradition.

Contemporary pagans and heathens generally follow a solar ritual year, divided into eight by the solstices, equinoxes, and cross-quarter days between them. Some groups incorporate these solar markers with full moons, as in the *Esbats* and *Sabbats* of certain present-day denominations of witchcraft. However, these are somewhat modern constructs.

But as P. D. Brown demonstrates here through numerous historical records and ancient texts, the lunar months (or moons) of the year were of fundamental significance in ancient Germanic and Norse religious observance. This plentiful evidence indicates that the major Norse sacrificial feasts of *Dísablót*, Yule, Þorrablót, *Disting*, and *Sigrblót* are all lunar-related festivals. *Thirteen Moons* also presents a series of original poems intended to be recited outdoors at each of the thirteen moons.

This work of impeccable scholarship represents a major step forwards in the study of these important traditions. It will be a revelation to many.

—**Nigel Pennick**, author of over fifty books on traditional European folklore, customs, and beliefs

Thirteen Moons is a slender but magnificent achievement of a rare sort. It starts with a solid scholarly look at the source texts and adds the Mead of Poetry in abundance, so that all who read it may live and enact the thirteen moons with inspiring and meaningful poetic rituals in today's world. A much-needed reconnection with the natural and spiritual life of our ancestors.

—**Eirik Westcoat**, author of *Eagle's Mead* and *Viking Poetry for Heathen Rites*

In *Thirteen Moons*, P. D. Brown shows us how we can more accurately determine the dates of heathen celebrations according to the historical source material. By taking into consideration the differences in ~~the S~~ runic dating sticks, and much more, he

arguments which offer new perspectives on the dating of the main holy festivals such as *Disting*, *Dísablót*, Yule, *Sigrblót*, and *Þorrablót*. This is a must-have for anyone interested in pursuing the *true* Old Ways of the heathen world.

—**Scott T. Shell, PhD**, author of *The Application of Peircean Semiotics to the Elder Futhark Tradition: Establishing Parameters of Magical Communication*, and founder of the *Continental Germanic Heathenry* YouTube channel

Some might dismiss those who insist on a current and academically critical interpretation of the pre-Christian Nordic lunisolar calendar as being simple bean-counters, fixated on technicalities. After all, time reckoning itself is mechanical, and calendars are just tools whose value is contingent upon their functionality.

Personally, though, I think that it is *through* such technicalities that the mysteries emerge. And to complement this particular machine and really get it up and running, we also must have art. We need poetry and stories that sideline the mechanical and connect it to the vernacular.

P. D. Brown pulls no punches when it comes to common delusions that we have all been guilty of harboring about ancient timekeeping in the North. Instead of the naive romance that has often prevailed until now, he offers an abundance of what is needed: *well-informed artistry*. Through links like this we may begin to reenter mythic time: to make the Eternal Return.

—**Eirik Storesund**, creator and host of the *Brute Norse* podcast

The moon is a mysterious body. Experiencing its role in our tradition is a powerful tool in individual development. To have a guide in this experience like P. D. Brown—a master wordsmith deeply familiar with the essence of the topic—is a priceless gift.

—**Edred Thorsson**, founder of the Rune-Gild and author of *The Nine Doors of Midgard: A Curriculum of Rune-Work*

Thirteen Moons

Other works by P. D. Brown

Poetry:
A Crown of Runes
Dark Fruit of an Ash
The Rune Poems: A Reawakened Tradition
(co-editor and contributor)

Prose Tales:
The Hidden Door

Recordings:
The Battle of the Trees
Fire & Ice
At Saga's Stream
Swan-Song and Swan Maidens
Three Tales of the Island of Britain

For more on the work of P. D. Brown, visit:
www.facebook.com/halfmanhalfmyth
www.scop.co.uk

Thirteen Moons
Reflections on the Heathen Lunar Year

P. D. Brown

Thirteen Moons: Reflections on the Heathen Lunar Year
by P. D. Brown

First published in 2022 by Gilded Books.
Edited by Michael Moynihan.
Typeset by Joshua Buckley.
Cover design by Joshua Buckley in collaboration with Antumnos Studio.
Gilded Books colophon and lettering by Luke Tromiczak.
Cover painting: *L'Hiver* (Winter) by Alexandre Calame, 1851. Digital treatment by
Antumnos Studio.
Copyright © 2022 P. D. Brown.
ISBN: 978-1-95-9353-00-3 (Paperback)
ISBN: 978-1-95-9353-01-0 (Ebook - Kindle)

Author's Acknowledgements
I am grateful to several individuals for their erudition in helping me to understand these
matters: Garrick Wells, whose online article "The Secrets of Heathen Time Keeping"
first set me on this enquiry; Göran Henriksson, for his revelation of the Gamla Uppsala
alignments and for correcting my erroneous conflation of the *octaeteris* and lunar
standstills; Robert Sass, whose "Aldsidu" blog has been invaluable, as has been his
perseverance and patience in promoting the Germanic lunisolar calendar; Lohengrin von
Munsalväsche for explaining to me the peculiarities of the ancient Roman calendar and
the true reading of "*ǣrra*" and "*æftera*"; and, last but not least, Andreas Nordberg, whose
groundbreaking study I hope will one day be translated into English in its entirety. I also
owe thanks to Professor John McKinnell for granting permission to quote at length from
his material and for recommending several sources; Michael Moynihan for his attentive
editing and close translations of all the Old Norse/Icelandic texts that appear here; and
Josh Buckley for his careful design work.

Gilded Books / Arcana Europa Media
P.O. Box 6115
North Augusta, SC 29861
www.arcanaeuropamedia.com

CONTENTS

Preface: Shifting Tides of Sacrifice

The poems in this book were written with the idea that they can be spoken outdoors, standing before a full moon. What other ceremony, if any, that accompanies them is up to the speaker. Sometimes further verses suggest other actions, such as drinking or libating mead or beer, or lighting a fire. Whether or not these verses and their concomitant actions are performed is again, of course, entirely up to the speaker.

That offerings of fire were made to the gods is suggested in stanza 10 of the Eddic poem *Hyndluljóð* (The Lay of Hyndla), where the *hörg*, or altar, of Freyja's devotee, Óttarr, is said to have turned to glass, which could only be brought about through intense heat. Other practices are not attested in the sources that have come down to us, such as the offering of incense in the words for the *Álfablót* poem, and the offering of alcohol by libation upon the ground. I do not claim though that they are anything other than something I like to include. Indeed, the very practice of ceremonies at each and every full moon is not attested (although Tacitus's remarks in chapter 11 of his *Germania*, which I will discuss later, could be presented as evidence of regular gatherings).

One sort of offering I would never make, but which is historically attested, is blood sacrifice. The Old Norse word *blót*, usually translated as "sacrifice," is cognate with our modern word "blood." I do not eat meat, so I do not want to offer an animal's life. The only blood I would want to offer is the "Blood of Kvasir" in both its senses—as actual mead and as poetry. That's my personal position and I acknowledge it as such.

There is one practice that I do which seems to be almost wilfully ignored by the majority and that is the custom of performing certain rituals and ceremonies at the right time. The times of these rituals were reckoned by the moon. Two of them are the most mentioned in the sources: "Winter Nights," which is completely ignored by some and has simply become another name for Halloween with most; and Yule, which is practised but—in my considered but not received opinion—at the wrong time. I therefore begin with an explanation of when these and other lunar festivals would have taken place and how the times of their observance can again be calculated.

P. D. Brown
Cloverlea
2022

Introduction:
Moonlight Breaks through the Fog

I have read many of the sagas that are available in translation. I have read the *Poetic Edda*, the *Prose Edda*, and *Heimskringla*, the latter being a history of the kings of Norway by Snorri Sturluson. Nowhere in this literature have I ever come across a phrase such as "it was the eve of the longest day" or "a great feast was held to celebrate the longest night" or "it was the time of equal day and equal night and, as was the custom, sacrifices were to be held."[1] The festivals most often mentioned are Winter Nights (*vetrnætr*) and Yule (*jól*).

I do not think the solstices and equinoxes were religious festivals that were celebrated by the Germanic peoples before their conversion, whether they spoke Old Norse, Old English, or Old Saxon. They would have been aware of when these days were but, for reasons I will come to, the solstices and equinoxes would at best have been mere markers for their ritual calendar year, which would have been a lunisolar calendar.

Why is such a view contrary to what the vast majority of modern heathens believe? How did they come to think that the solstices, equinoxes, and often as well the "quarter-day" festivals falling roughly halfway in between those four solar days, comprised the ritual year of the Norse and Saxon cultures?

---

1. Snorri does mention the equinoxes in the *Skáldskaparmál* and he refers to midsummer in *Heimskringla*; I shall discuss these below in the "*Sigrblót*" section, pp. 42–47.

1

Briefly stated, the answer seems to lie in the history of how modern heathenry developed in the latter half of the twentieth century. For a long time, if you wanted to be a Pagan and join something, there was Wicca.[2] Then for a time the nearest thing you could get to a heathen group, in Britain at least, was the "Seax-Wicca," where the names of the Lord and Lady, Cernunnos and Diana or whatever, were substituted with Woden and Frigg. There was naturally a carry-over of ideas as the gaps in people's knowledge were still wide. The Wiccan "Wheel of the Year" was carried across to those trying to create a heathen religion. It was all people knew. This was entirely understandable, as few then could access academic resources and there was no Internet. Oddly, however, it was not felt necessary to hold new moon or full moon ceremonies like Wicca does. The lunar cycle was largely ignored by all modern groups that connected themselves to Germanic heathen beliefs and traditions, with one notable exception—the Rune-Gild, which has since its founding in 1980 included a set of "Full Moon Rites" as part of its private ritual calendar.[3]

There is an idea amongst some Wiccans that witchcraft has survived in an unbroken line, a kind of pagan apostolic succession, since prehistory. Presumably Gerald Gardner and his co-founders thought this kind of continuity gave it the kudos of authenticity. It now seems likely that modern Wicca originated from a group of individuals whose secular interests included drama, astronomy, herbalism, nature poetry, and folklore; their esoteric interests included "the Golden Dawn and its offshoots; Co-Masonry; Theosophy; Druidry; astrology and Eastern disciplines such as yoga."[4] Some had evidently been members of the Golden Dawn, which explains the influence of this order's ritual in Wicca. Significantly, both the Golden Dawn and, later, Aleister Crowley's Thelema movement had ceremonies for the solstices and equinoxes.

2. For a detailed history of the development of modern Wicca in Britain, see Hutton, *The Triumph of the Moon*.

3. For the background on this group, see Thorsson, *History of the Rune-Gild*, which also discusses its history within the context of the larger Germanic revival.

4. Heselton, *In Search of the New Forest Coven*, 240.

Gardner did not need to make such claims of a continuous lineage stretching back into the ancient past. Modern Wicca stands on its own merits—and, for all its in-fighting, so does what has evolved into the modern revival of the pre-Christian religious practices of the Norse, Saxon, and Anglo-Saxon peoples. Yet many drawn to the worship of the gods of the pre-Christian Germanic peoples still make a similar error in claiming that the "Wheel of the Year" has an ancient pedigree.

There is nothing inherently wrong with celebrating the stations of the Wheel of the Year, only in maintaining that this is what Germanic heathens did in the past before the conversion, when there is no evidence to support this. Some would say, "But absence of evidence is not evidence of absence," displaying a currently popular specious logic. Actually, it is exactly that—evidence (not proof) of absence. Such people say it themselves: there is no evidence, there is an absence of evidence, to support their idea. In *Thirteen Moons*, I will present evidence for what I think to be the pre-Christian Germanic calendar.

There is a type of modern heathen who is frank enough to say they follow a modern Ásatrú that is just that—a *modern creation*. There is no duplicity, wilful or otherwise, in following such a path, and the Wheel of the Year has an understandable aesthetic and symmetrical appeal.

There are other modern heathens who maintain that they can believe anything they wish to and no one can deny the validity of their belief. To such people I can only say that if you want to believe that Sleipnir is a unicorn, that Bifröst is a "Rainbow Goddess," and the Wheel of the Year was "what the Vikings did," you can indeed believe that—just do not expect me to respect or conform to your belief for fear that you will be offended. I would rather root my practice in that for which there is evidence, and where I do not root my practice in that for which there is evidence, I will acknowledge it as something that works for me but has no precedent in what knowledge has come down to us.

Another way that some celebrate seasonal festivals is to wait until the seasons announce themselves by blackthorn buds blossoming, lambs being born, swallows arriving, hazelnuts ripening, salmon leaping, leaves falling, geese leaving, or snow falling. The great virtue of this system is that it is tied to what is happening in one's local landscape as our world orbits the sun. The elder flowers appear in Cornwall much earlier than they do in Cumbria, for example. I have always thought it incongruous to describe Lammas as a harvest festival; the harvest is rarely in by the first day of August, at least where I live. Using a localised system of "seasonal signs," you can even await the likelihood of a weather forecast being accurate and celebrate the start of summer on a hot day!

However, there are certain important festivals that seem to have been held on full moons in the past. Through researching such matters, many things have become clear to me: most importantly, these festivals were held according to a far older system of time-reckoning than the one we commonly use today, and that ancient system was based upon the lunar cycle. There are many clues in the extant medieval literature which enable us to reconstruct this older time-reckoning with confidence and increasing precision.

The high points and turning points of the ancient heathen calendar cannot—and should not—be forced to sit on arbitrary dates within the twelve months of our modern one. The old system works according to its own lights. If a festival was held on a particular phase of the moon, I think it should be today; the time was the occasion and the occasion was the time.

It was only recently, in 2020, that I ceased to celebrate Yule at the winter solstice as a result of my research into the ancient way of determining when such festivals took place. I do not feel embarrassed that I had been "getting it wrong" all these years. What would embarrass me is continuing in that error once I became aware of it. In the pages that follow, I will discuss what led me to the view that the heathen calendar was lunisolar in nature.

But there is another more arcane reason for taking the trouble to walk to a secluded spot beneath the bright moon on certain nights of the year. There is a definite change of atmosphere that occurs with the coming of the night in such places, and it is more than just the otherness that our diurnal instincts sense as dusk turns to darkness. In a world far removed from the static and artificial luminescence of streetlamps, the shifting and gentle light of the moon has a magic all of its own.

The Evidence for a Lunar Calendar and Ritual Year

The difficulty with lunar calendars is that they will vary wildly with our perceptions of what constitutes "midsummer," "midwinter," and the "new year." This is because we have been culturally tied for centuries to a twelve-month solar calendar.

Ancient Germanic heathens (and Celts too) reckoned a day not from dawn to dawn or from midnight to midnight, but from sunset to sunset. The onset of dusk began a new "day," or rather a new twenty-four-hour cycle. This is why we still speak of "May Eve," "Christmas Eve," and so forth. Time was measured in nights. In modern England a survival of this way of reckoning time is still evident in the term "fortnight,"[1] which is used to denote a period of fourteen days or two weeks.

Snorri gives us mythical evidence of this in the *Prose Edda* text *Gylfaginning* (The Tricking of Gylfi), §9:

> *Þá tók Alfǫðr Nótt ok Dag son hennar ok gaf þeim tvá hesta ok tvær kerrur ok setti þau upp á himin at þau skulu ríða á hverjum tveim dægrum umhverfis jǫrðina. Ríðr Nótt fyrri þeim hesti er kallaðr er Hrímfaxi.*

Then Allfather (Óðinn) took Night and Day, her son, and gave

---

1. Deriving from Old English *fēowertīene niht*, "fourteen nights."

them two horses and two chariots, and set them up in the sky so that they have to ride for each pair of twelve-hour periods around the Earth. Night rides for the first of these (periods) on the horse which is called Hrímfaxi.[2]

Thus, the twelve-hour period of Nótt (Night) is seen as preceding that of Dag (Day). The Old Icelandic term *dægr* referred generically to either of the two twelve-hour periods (corresponding roughly to "nighttime" and "daytime") that together make up a twenty-four-hour cycle, or "day," in our modern, solar-based conception.

More directly, in his first-century ethnographic treatise *Germania* (chapter 11), Tacitus states about the Germanic peoples in general:

nec dierum numerum, ut nos, sed noctium computant. sic constituunt, sic condicunt: nox ducere diem videtur.

They do not reckon time by days, as we do, but by nights. All their engagements and appointments are made on this system. Night is regarded as ushering in the day.[3]

Today we tend to count days by the rising and setting of that luminary of the day, the sun. How then, in ancient times, were larger numbers of nights to be reckoned? The answer is clearly by that luminary of the night, the moon. But the moon can rise or set during the day too, and at more widely varying times. So the measuring of nights was from the regular phases of the moon, one lunation, from a new moon to a new moon for example (thus giving us the word "month"). These lunations were used to count up a year. In stanza 14 of the Eddic poem *Alvíssmál* (The Lay of Alvíss), we are told: "*Máni heitir með mǫnnum, . . . kalla álfar ártala*"

---

2. Old Icelandic text in Snorri, *Edda: Prologue and Gylfaginning* (ed. Faulkes), 13; translation by Michael Moynihan.

3. Latin text in Tacitus, *Germania* (ed. Furneaux), 60; English from *Germania* (trans. Mattingly and Handford), 110.

("Moon it's called among men, . . . elves call it year-tallier").[4]

By contrast, stanza 16, which relates various names for the sun, makes no reference to the marking of time. However, stanza 23 of the Eddic poem *Vafþrúðnismál* (The Lay of Vafþrúðnir) does mention the sun:

> *Mundilferi heitir,   hann er Mána faðir,*
>   *ok svá Sólar it sama;*
> *himin hverfa   þau skolo hverian dag,*
>   *ǫldom at ártali.*

> Mundilfari he is called, he is the father of Máni (Moon),
> and likewise of Sól (Sun);
> through the sky they must spin every day,
> as a year-tallier for men.[5]

As we shall see, the sun does have a function in a lunisolar calendar. However, stanza 25, lines 3–4, again has the moon alone as the counter of years:

> *ný ok nið   skopo nýt regin,*
>   *ǫldom at ártali.*

> Waxing moon and waning moon the Ruling Powers shaped
> for men as a year-tallier.[6]

Similarly, in Snorri's treatise *Skáldskaparmál* (The Language of Poetry), when he provides lists of poetical names for various things, under Moon (*tungl*), we again find "year-tallier" (*ártali*).[7] The names for the sun which Snorri provides have none that indicate a time-keeping function.

---

4. Old Icelandic from *Edda* (ed. Neckel), I, 122; trans. Moynihan.
5. Old Icelandic from *Edda* (ed. Neckel), I, 47; trans. Moynihan.
6. Old Icelandic from *Edda* (ed. Neckel), I, 47; trans. Moynihan.
7. Snorri, *Edda: Skáldskaparmál* (ed. Faulkes), I, 85.

Sacrificial Feasts in the Lunar Calendar

We will now have a more in-depth look at those sacrificial feasts or festivals for which there is evidence that they were tied to particular "moons" or months of the year. The first three of these feasts all take place in winter; the fourth marks the beginning of summer. They are the ones that are mentioned in the sagas and elsewhere.

Winter Nights

Of especial interest is the following quotation from the Anglo-Saxon poem *Beowulf*, lines 146b–48a:

> . . . *Wæs sēo hwīl micel:*
> *twelf wintra tīd   torn ġeþolode*
> *wine Scyldinga*

This went on for a long time: for a period of twelve years the Scyldings' friend suffered affliction.[1]

Old English *tīd* means "time, period, era." It is the source of modern English "tide" (as in "Yuletide," "wintertide", etc.)[2] and is cognate with the Dutch word *tijd* and German *Zeit,* both meaning "time." The above

---

1. Old English from the fourth edition of Klaeber, ed., *Beowulf,* 8. English from *Beowulf* (trans. Swanton), 40.

2. The now primary sense of "tide" as relating to the ebbing and flowing of the sea dates from late Middle English.

quotation from *Beowulf* illustrates how, just as twenty-four-hour periods were reckoned in nights, so too were years reckoned in winters. The translator has rendered *twelf wintra tīd* as "for a period of twelve years."

In the Old Norse dictionary compiled by Cleasby and Vigfusson, a secondary meaning is provided in the entry for the word *vetr* (winter), stating that it denotes "*a year*; as in A. S. [Anglo-Saxon] days were reckoned by nights, so years were counted in winters." We may also note that the compound noun *vetrar-tungl* is defined as "the winter moon, the moon when winter sets in."[3]

We see, then, that the year began in winter and at a certain moon, which in Old Norse was known as *vetrnætr*, "the winter nights, the three days which begin the winter season."[4] Although there is nothing in the sources directly stating that the Norse festival of the Winter Nights (*vetrnætr*) was held over a full moon, I think most likely that it would have corresponded to the three nights when the moon was fullest. More than a millennia earlier, Tacitus remarks (*Germania*, chap. 11) of the Germanic tribes in general:

> *coëunt, nisi quid fortuitum et subitum incidit, certis diebus, cum aut incohatur luna aut impletur; nam agendis rebus hoc auspicatissiumum initium credunt.*

> Except in the case of accident or emergency, they assemble on certain particular days, either shortly after the new moon or shortly before the full moon. These, they hold, are the most auspicious days for embarking upon any enterprise.[5]

Admittedly, the material I am quoting from Tacitus's *Germania* derives from a reference far removed in time and place to the Scandinavia of the

---

3. See Cleasby and Vigfusson, *An Icelandic-English Dictionary*, under "*vetr*" and "*vetrartungl*."

4. Cleasby and Vigfusson, *An Icelandic-English Dictionary*, under "*vetrnætr*."

5. Latin text in Tacitus, *Germania* (ed. Furneaux), 59–60; English from *Germania* (trans. Mattingly and Handford), 110.

sagas. We cannot claim that there is a "Pan-Germanic culture" displaying a marked conformity across the broad diaspora of those speaking Germanic languages in the pre-Christian era. However, there are parallels, explored in this essay, to do with measuring time. Broader considerations are also of relevance here.

Many cultures across the world used, and still use, lunar observances. The traditional Chinese, Jewish, and Muslim calendars are all lunar, and even the Romans originally had a lunar calendar. The beginning and end of Ramadan, the ninth month of the Muslim year (and the time of fasting), is marked by a new moon, the latter announcing the holiday of Eid. Each year Eid changes date according to the Gregorian calendar by around eleven days because the lunar year has 354 days. The Islamic calendar is thus a purely lunar calendar, whereas many others, including the traditional Hindu calendars, are lunisolar, which is to say, the stations of the sun are observed (rather than celebrated as festivals) as a way of keeping the lunar and solar years synchronised in some way. This also appears to have been the case with the Anglo-Saxon calendar, which we will consider in more detail below.

Tacitus states the new moon was important as well as the full moon, so why not have the new moon as a focus for festivals? A practical consideration is to have as much moonlight as possible available not only during a festival but also for the nights before and after. This would be important for travelling to and from any gathering, especially at higher latitudes where winter nights are longer.

In chapter 10 of *Gísla saga Súrssonar* (Gísli's Saga), we find the following:

> *Ok líðr nú svá sumarit, ok kømr at vetrnáttum. Þat var þá margra manna siðr at fagna vetri í þann tíma, ok hafa þá veizlur ok vetrnáttablót.*

And now the summer passes in this way, and comes to Winter Nights. It was the custom then of many men to make a feast at that time for the onset of winter, and to hold banquets and

Winter Nights' sacrifices.[6]

Dísablót

Dísablót is a sacrifice mentioned in several sagas, for example in the *Ynglinga saga* (The Saga of the Ynglings; found in Snorri's *Heimskringla*), *Egils saga* (The Saga of Egill Skallagrímsson), and *Hervarar saga ok Heiðreks* (The Saga of Hervör and Heiðrek). In chapter 6 of *Víga-Glúms saga* (The Saga of Víga-Glúm), we learn that *dísablót* fell on Winter Nights:

> *Þar var veizla búin at vetrnóttum ok gert dísablót, ok allir skulu þessa minning gera.*

> There a feast was held on Winter Nights and a *dísablót* was done, and everyone was obligated to make this remembrance.[7]

A *dísablót* means a "sacrifice to the *dísir*." Who the *dísir* were is not entirely clear; they appear to have been female ancestral spirits but on a generalised level.

The *Þiðrandra þáttr ok Þorhalls* (Tale of Þiðrandi and Þórhall), a short story found in the late fourteenth-century *Flateyjarbók* manuscript, also has the *dísir* appearing at Winter Nights. Here the *dísir* arrive on horseback, where one character says of them to his host: "I can guess that they were not women but the fetches that follow your family."[8] Two groups of *dísir* arrive, and one group kills the host's son, Þiðrandi, showing that the *dísir* could be malevolent when displeased, as is implied also in the death of Aðils, discussed below (where a horse again also features).

Some have seen the *dísir* as related to the cult of the *matronae*, or Matrons, who were worshipped in regions of southern Germany and elsewhere, and are known to us from Roman votive monuments

---

6. *Gísla saga Súrssonar* (ed. Jónsson), 23; trans. Moynihan.

7. *Víga-Glúms saga* (ed. Turville-Petre), 9; trans. Moynihan.

8. Quoted in Gunnell, "The Season of the *Dísir*," 133.

dedicated to them.[9] A further connection can be drawn to the rites of Mothers' Night mentioned by Bede (discussed below). Again, we have three things linked tenuously by the common denominator of divine or supernatural mother beings from places distinct in time and place, but linked nonetheless. That the *matronae* are thought to be of Celtic origin by some seems rather at odds with a Germanic ancestral cult. Here I can do no better than quote at length from *Meeting the Other in Norse Myth and Legend* by John McKinnell:

> There is, however, abundant evidence that dead female relatives *in general* were venerated in the pre-Christian Germanic world. Votive stones and altars from the Roman period dedicated to the *matronae* or *matres* are common on the lower Rhine, in eastern Gaul and in upper Italy. They may have Celtic origins and could have originated amongst the mixed Celtic-Germanic populations on the lower Rhine, but the majority include Germanic names. Dedications include *matribus Suebis* 'to the Suebian mothers', *matribus Frisivis paternis* 'to the Frisian mothers on [my] father's side', *matribus germanis* (probably 'to the mothers related [to me]'). . . . The cult itself may have existed before and/or after the Roman period; de Vries suggests that in southern Germany, it survived long enough to be Christianised into the veneration of the Three Holy Virgins, whose cult was in place by 1028.
>
> Most stones depict three *matronae* sitting or standing side by side, at least one of whom has a basket of fruit in her lap. Sometimes the central one looks like an unmarried woman, with loose hair and a garland, while the other two have headdresses which suggest they are married women. The fruit and other attributes often carved alongside them suggest that they were invoked for fertility, but most of those who erected the stones

---

9. For more on the *matronae*, see the relevant entries in Simek, *Dictionary of Northern Mythology*, 204–8, et passim (regarding individual Matron names); and the section on "Die Vielzahl der weiblichen Gottheiten (Matronen, Disen, Nornen, Walküren)" in Simek, *Religion und Mythologie der Germanen*, 117–28.

seem to have been soldiers, and a few names of *matronae* suggest that they could be invoked for protection in war. There is no evidence that they represent *individual* dead relatives of their worshippers.

Bede's *De Temporum Ratione* [The Reckoning of Time] ch. 15 (written in 725), refers to a heathen Anglo-Saxon festival called *modranect* 'night of the mothers', which he says was the heathen new year, celebrated on what is now Christmas Day and involving unspecified nocturnal rituals. We do not know whether these aimed to secure help from female ancestors or to placate them, but they may represent a continuation of the worship of the *matronae*. There may be further evidence for this in the *First Merseburg Charm*, whose tenth-century manuscript probably comes from Fulda, central Germany. The charm itself is doubtless older, but [Gerhard] Eis's confidence in dating it to the third or fourth century (solely because of its resemblance to the cult of the *matronae*) seems misplaced. It reads:

> Eiris sazun idisi   sazun hera duoder.
> Suma hapt heptidun,   suma hers lezidun,
> suma clubodun   umbi cuoniouuidi.
> Insprinc haptbandum   inuar uigandun!

In l. 1, *hera duoder* is problematic: the line should clearly alliterate on a vowel and *duoder* is obscure. Eis therefore amends to *era muoder* 'honoured mothers' and translates:

> 'Long ago the Idisi sat down, the honoured mothers sat down.
> Some bound bonds, some held back the army,
> Some split around the fetters.
> Spring out of imprisoning bonds, escape from warriors!'

He also points to the south German gloss *matrona : itis*, and to Old English *ides* 'lady'. Bede's *modranect* and the *idisi* probably reflect a concept similar to that of the Germanic Latin *matres* or *matronae*. The *First Merseburg Charm* gives them three functions: binding, hindering enemy armies and releasing from bonds. They may also have been called upon to ensure crop and human fertility, perhaps particularly at the beginning of a new year.

This recalls the pre-Christian Norse festival of *dísablót*, which is mentioned in *Víga-Glúms saga* ch. 6. Old High German *idis*, Old English *ides* and Old Norse *dís* are probably related, although the Old English noun has lost most of its supernatural connotations. According to *Víga-Glúms saga*, the *dísablót* was held *at vetrnóttum* 'at the winter nights', the official beginning of winter, the first of the year's two seasons. It appears from *Ynglinga saga*, where King Aðils is accidentally killed while riding round the *dísasalr* [recte: *dísarsalr*], that the *dísir* could harm their devotees as well as help them. The association of *dísir* with 'dead women' in *Atlamál* 28 again suggests that they were dead female relatives. In *Hervarar saga ok Heiðriks* ch. 7, Heiðrekr's wife Helga is so infuriated when her husband kills her father that she hangs herself in the *dísasalr*, possibly in order to become a malevolent *dís*.[10]

Dísablót may have been held in early spring in Sweden. In chapter 29 of the *Ynglinga saga*, Snorri relates:

> Aðils konungr var at dísablóti ok reið hesti um dísar-salinn; hestrinn drap fótum undir honum ok fell ok konungr af fram, ok kom hǫfuð hans á stein, svá at haussinn brotnaði, en heilinn lá á steininum; þat var hans bani; hann dó at Upsǫlum ok er þar heygðr.

King Aðils was sacrificing to the *dísir* and rode his horse around

10. McKinnell, *Meeting the Other in Norse Myth and Legend*, 198–200; quoted by kind permission of the author.

the *dís*'s hall; the horse stumbled beneath him, over its feet, and the king too fell straight ahead, and his head hit a rock so that his skull fractured and his brains lay upon the rock; that was his bane. He died at Uppsala and is buried there in a mound.[11]

In contrast to the term *dísablót*, which refers to the worship of *dísir* goddesses (plural), the word describing Aðils's hall is *dísar-salr*, which uses the singular form. There appears to be just a single *dís* within the shrine, perhaps Aðils's family's ancestress.

Terry Gunnell's article "The Season of the *Dísir*" tells us of an early mediaeval Swedish legal tract, *Upplandslagen* (the Law of Uppland). The tract mentions a legal assembly (*þing*) called the *disæþing* ("*þing* of the *disir*"), and states that this gathering was also the occasion of a longstanding market, which Snorri informs us (*Óláfs saga helga* [St. Olaf's Saga], chap. 77) is associated with religious rites:

> Í Svíþjóðu var þat forn landz-siðr, meðan heiðni var þar, at hǫfuðblót skyldi vera at Upsǫlum at gói; skyldi þá blóta til friðar ok sigrs konungi sínum, ok skyldu menn þangat sœkja um alt Svíaveldi. . . . En nú síðan er kristni var alsiða í Svíþjóð, en konungar afrœkðusk at sitja at Upsǫlum, þá var fœrðr markaðrinn ok hafðr kyndilmessu; . . . Er þar þing Svía, ok sœkja þeir þar til um alt land.

In Sweden it was the old custom of the land, whilst heathenism was practised there, that the main sacrifice had to be held at Uppsala in the month of *Gói* [15th of February till the 15th of March]. They had to sacrifice then to peace and victory for their king, and people from the whole Swedish kingdom had to come there. . . . But now ever since Christianity was the general custom in Sweden, and the kings ceased to reside at Uppsala, then the market was shifted and held at Candlemas [2nd February]; . . . The legal assembly (*þing*) of the Swedes is there, and they come

---

11. Snorri, *Heimskringla* (ed. Jónsson), I, 56; trans. Moynihan.

to it from all over the land.[12]

In different parts of Scandinavia, sacrifices to Freyr may have been more important at Winter Nights. *Ynglinga saga* (chap. 8) has:

Þá skyldi blóta í móti vetri til árs . . .

Then at the onset of winter, a sacrifice should be made for a good season . . .[13]

Also, in *Gísla saga Súrssonar* (chap. 15), we read:

Þorgrímr ætlaði at hafa haustboð at vetr nóttum ok fagna vetri ok blóta Frey.

Þorgrímr intended to have an autumn banquet at Winter Nights and celebrate the onset of winter and make a sacrifice to Freyr.[14]

We know from stanza 5 of the Eddic poem *Grímnismál* (The Lay of Grímnir) that Freyr ruled over *Álfheimr* (Elf-home). The *álfablót* (sacrifice to the elves) is another offering which seems to have taken place in autumn and if one were honouring Freyr, it would be an appropriate time to honour those he ruled over, too.

The skald Sigvatr Þórðarson's poem *Austrfararvísur* (Verses on a Journey to the East) tells of a diplomatic mission to Sweden that appears to have been undertaken in autumn and which he accompanied. Some believe such a journey would have been better undertaken in the spring and cite stanza 10's mention of spring. The poem also refers to *álfablót*. I quote the stanzas of interest:[15]

---

12. Snorri, *Heimskringla* (ed. Jónsson), II, 134; trans. Moynihan. Also see Gunnell, "The Season of the *Dísir*," 133–35.

13. Snorri, *Heimskringla* (ed. Jónsson), I, 20; trans. Moynihan.

14. *Gísla saga Súrssonar* (ed. Jónsson), 36; trans. Moynihan.

15. In these English translations, several notations help to show the intricate system of

Stanza 1:
Hugstóra biðk heyra
hressfærs jǫfurs, þessar
—þolðak vás— hvé vísur,
verðung, of fǫr gerðak.
Sendr vask upp af ǫndrum
austr (svafk fátt í hausti)
til Svíþjóðar (síðan)
svanvangs í fǫr langa.

I ask the mighty-hearted retinue of the energetic ruler [Óláfr] to hear how I composed these verses about a journey; I endured hardship. I was sent up from the skis of the swan-plain [SEA > SHIPS] on a long journey east to Sweden; I slept little after that in the autumn.

Stanza 5:
"Gakkat inn," kvað ekkja,
"armi drengr, en lengra;
hræðumk ek við Óðins
—erum heiðin vér— reiði."
Rýgr kvazk inni eiga
óþekk, sús mér hnekkði,
alfablót, sem ulfi
ótvín, í bœ sínum.

"Do not come any farther in, wretched fellow," said the woman; "I fear the wrath of Óðinn; we are heathen." The disagreeable

---

kennings and referents that is employed by the skaldic poet. In the translation of stanza 1, for example, there appears the phrase "the skis of the swan-plain [SEA > SHIPS]." Here the square brackets indicate who or what is ultimately being referred to, while the arrow shows the relationship between a kenning's base word or phrase (in this case, "skis") and the determinant ("of the swan-plain"). Thus, realising that the swan's plain is the sea, the listener or reader can make the imaginative leap and know that the "skis" of the sea are ships.

female, who drove me away like a wolf without hesitation, said they were holding a sacrifice to the elves inside her farmhouse.

Stanza 10:
Snjalls létum skip skolla
skjǫldungs við ey tjǫlduð
fyr ágætu úti
ǫndvert sumar landi.
Enn í haust, es hestar
hagþorns á mó sporna
(ték ýmissar) Ekkils,
(íðir) hlýtk at ríða.

We let the ship of the valiant monarch [Óláfr] skulk with its awnings up at the beginning of summer out by an island opposite some excellent country. But it is my lot to ride in autumn, when the horses of Ekkill <sea-king> [SHIPS] tread on the hawthorn's moor [LAND]; I report various doings.[16]

Stanza 1 seems straightforward enough: he slept little in the autumn because he was enduring a hard journey. Stanza 10's meaning to me is simply something of a complaint along the lines of "So, when summer began and the weather was good, the king's ship lay idle. Now it's too risky to sail, the king's ships have been hauled on land and I have to travel in autumn, on horseback." Therefore, I am not convinced that the journey must have happened in spring purely because the weather would have been better. (As I write this, in Scotland on Easter Monday, 5th April, 2021, sleet and snow, driven by winds of fifty miles per hour, fly horizontally past the window, and make me think such a notion to be not necessarily the case at all.)

Quite possibly, then, we have three religious activities happening at Winter Nights: sacrifices to the *dísir*, to the *álfar*, and to Freyr. Not

16. Text and translation from R. D. Fulk, ed., "Sigvatr Þórðarson, *Austrfararvísur*," in Whaley, ed., *Poetry from the Kings' Sagas* 1, I, 578.

all three may have been practised by everyone, but over a three-night period there would have been time for all three. I see the Winter Night's full moon as the "lunar new year" because their years commenced with the onset of darkness in autumn. In Scotland, Quarter-Days (days that began each quarter of the year, for legal purposes, for example, when rents fell due) still fall in November, February, May, and August, but due to changing from the Julian to the Gregorian calendar, the actual days are 11th November, 2nd February, 15th May, and 2nd August. Such dates may well have originally been full or new moons, but became fixed in a solar calendar. (I think it likely that the Celtic festival of Samhain,[17] which falls around 1st November and also features strong supernatural happenings and the dead, was originally a lunar new year festival too.) The second moon of winter does not have any particular festivities associated with it.

The earliest references to seasonal festivals are not in Snorri's *Heimskringla*, written around 1220, but rather the *Ágrip af Nóregskonungasögum* (Summary of the Sagas of the Kings of Norway), which is slightly older and dates from late twelfth century. In this text we are told how Óláfr Tryggvason, the evangelising king who ruled over Norway circa 995–1000 CE,

> removed heathen sacrifices (*blót*) and drinking connected with the sacrifices, and instead got the common people to take up festive drinking at Christmas, Easter, St. John's Eve, and . . . Michaelsmass.[18]

No mention is made of when the heathen sacrifices originally had taken place. A commonly held belief in modern Paganism is that Yule was on the winter solstice and that the Christians "stole" the solstice and turned it into Christmas. This cannot be inferred from the above quote; taking up festive drinking at Christmas implies no change of practice (drinking)

17. The name may have meant "Summer's End," thus signifying the onset of the darker half of the year.

18. Quoted in Gunnell, "The Season of the *Dísir*," 123.

but does imply a change of date.

I propose now to look at the whole vexed question of the midwinter festivities, with reference mainly to two quotes in Snorri's *Heimskringla*, but more importantly to Bede's *De tempore ratione*.

Yule

The *Ynglinga saga*, chapter 8, has the following crucial information on Old Norse festivals:

> *Þá skyldi blóta í móti vetri til árs, en at miðjum vetri blóta til gróðrar, it þriðja at sumri, þat var sigrblót.*

> Then at the onset of winter, a sacrifice should be made for a good season; and in the middle of winter, a sacrifice for growth of crops; and a third one at summer, which was a sacrifice for victory (*sigrblót*).[19]

The beginning of winter festival would be the Winter Nights discussed above. The one "in the middle of winter" was the old festival of Yule (*jól*).

In our modern world, we are so used to thinking about time within a solar frame of reference that we immediately think of midwinter as the solstice—before the solstice, the nights are getting longer and after the solstice, the nights become shorter; the solstice is the middle of the dark season of winter. Midwinter in a lunar calendar is not the winter solstice; time is measured, as we have seen, by reference to the moon, yet the solstice has a role to play.

Óláfr Tryggvason was not the first ruler to move festivals. Although the *Ágrip Nóregskonungasögum* is older than *Heimskringla*, the latter gives the history of a king of Norway who reigned earlier than Óláfr Tryggvason. This was Hákon the Good (ruled 920–960 CE). One of this king's nicknames was Hákon Aðalsteinsfóstri; he was raised as a Christian in England as a foster son of Æthelstan, king of Wessex and Mercia. In chapter 13 of the *Saga Hákonar góða* (Saga of Hákon the Good), Snorri

19. Snorri, *Heimskringla* (ed. Jónsson), I, 20; trans. Moynihan.

tells us:

> *hann setti þat í lǫgum, at hefja jólahald þann tíma, sem kristnir*
> *menn . . . en áðr var jólahald hafit hǫku-nótt, þat var miðsvetrar-*
> *nótt, haldin iii.-nátta-jól.*

[King Hákon] had it set down in the laws that the keeping of Yule
was to begin at the same time as (is the custom) with Christians.
. . . previously, the keeping of Yule was celebrated on *hǫku-nótt,*[20]
that was midwinter's night, and lasted for three nights of Yule.[21]

Evidently, he did not have a long-term success with this or Óláfr would
not have had to repeat the stratagem.

As mentioned earlier, for a long time people have assumed that Yule
must have been on the solstice, and that Hákon and Óláfr moved Yule to
Christmas and "hijacked" the winter festival. Some have also thought that
Christmas was originally on the solstice, but if that was the case—which
it never was, as is explained below in this chapter—and Yule was on the
solstice, there would not have been any need to move it. The remark that
Yule "lasted for three nights" shows it had the same duration as Winter
Nights and again suggests the full of the moon.

Andreas Nordberg's work *Jul, disting och förkyrklig tideräkning:*
Kalendrar och kalendariska riter i det förkristna Norden (Yule, Disting,
and Pre-Julian Time-Reckoning: Calendars and Calendric Rituals in
Pre-Christian Scandinavia) includes a discussion of two ancient lunar
months, the first of which is referred to in Swedish as *Jultungel* (Yule
moon) and the second as *Disa, Distungel,* or *Distingstungel* (Dis-thing's
moon). The earliest record of the "Yule moon" dates from thirteenth-
century Iceland, where it was attested as *jóla tungl* (Yule's Moon), while
the name *Distingstungel* is attested from the mid sixteenth century in
the Dalecarlian dialects of central Sweden. Nordberg argues that these

---

20. The term "*hǫku-nótt*" is synonymous here with "midwinter's night," but the etymology
of "*hǫku*" remains unclear; see Nordberg, *Jul, disting och förkyrklig tideräkning,* 119–24.

21. Snorri, *Heimskringla* (ed. Jónsson), I, 185; trans. Moynihan.

lunar months are remnants of a pre-Christian system of time-reckoning, with the *Jultungel* connected to the pre-Christian feast of Yule and the *Distingstungel* being linked to a *dísir*-sacrifice at Uppsala. He sees the *Jultungel* as being related to the old Germanic month names: *Ýlir* and *Jólmánuðr* in Old Norse, the Anglo-Saxon *Giuli* and *Geola*, and the Gothic *Jiuleis*.

Nordberg then argues that two calendars were used in Scandinavia before the introduction of the Julian calendar. One seems similar to the week-calendar that was later used in Iceland; the other was lunisolar. Nordberg asserts that, according to the pre-Christian lunisolar calendar, the Yule celebration took place at the first full moon after the first new moon following the winter solstice, and—using the same method of calculation—the *Disting* took place at the third full moon. Nordberg makes the crucial point that in a lunisolar calendar, the winter solstice is important for keeping the solar and lunar years aligned, but the solstice was not Yule.

To further elucidate this point, we will consider the writings of the Venerable Bede. However, before we do, I should perhaps look at another calendar which, like all the others, has muddied the waters. Although this calendar is now unique to Iceland, Nordberg provides evidence it may be a vestige of an earlier system that was more widely used in Scandinavian and Baltic areas. It is still a workable calendar, but it is a solar calendar and is not related to the phases of the moon. I think that, originally, the first Icelandic settlers would have used a lunar calendar—but living so far north, the moon is lower in the sky, the weather cloudier, and the long hours of daylight in spring and summer all conspire to make the moon harder to see. Possibly for these reasons, in 930 CE they adopted a year of 52 weeks (52 x 7 = 364 days); this was comprised of twelve thirty-day months; 12 x 30 = only 360 days so they added four days to the summer, making 364 days. In 955 CE it was decided to introduce an extra week in summer every seventh year so that over a seven-year period, the average year length would be 365 days. By 1000 CE, the number of leap years made it necessary to meet for the annual Althing assembly after ten weeks instead of nine. The Icelanders were adroit enough to see and make amendments to this calendar—and to spot problems with the Julian calendar when the Church introduced it to Iceland and at which time the Icelanders adapted the week-calendar to the Julian calendar (and later to the Gregorian calendar). All of these problems, which we still resolve with our modern leap years, are solar-calendar issues.

Þorrablót

Þorrablót was a sacrificial midwinter festival. It was abolished during the Christianisation of Iceland but resurrected in the nineteenth century as a midwinter celebration. The timing for the festival coincides with the Icelandic calendar month of *Þorri*, which begins on the first Friday after 19th January. As we have seen, the basic "unit" of the calendar is the seven-day week. There are fifty-two weeks in an old Icelandic calendrical year (364 days). Every so often, a leap week is inserted so such a year has fifty-three weeks. Each year has a complete number of weeks with no days left over, and consequently every year begins on the same day of the week and each month will also begin on its own day of the week every year. For example, at the time of writing, in January 2021 CE, the next Icelandic month of *Þorri* will begin on the first Friday after the Gregorian calendar's 19th January, so by Gregorian reckoning, *Þorri* can commence on the first Friday that occurs between the 19th and 26th January. The year is divided into twelve months of thirty days, with four extra days added to summer (or eleven extra days in Icelandic leap years).

The month before *Þorri* is called *Jólmánuðr* (Yule-month). It starts on the Wednesday occurring between the 20th to the 27th December in the Gregorian calendar. This is evidence that the Icelanders here were following the precept of the evangelical King Hákon the Good and had moved Yule to Christmas, an alteration their forebears would have made through their continued interaction with Norway. That *Þorrablót* is described as a midwinter feast perhaps indicates that this old heathen feast was the lunar midwinter and was originally the same as Yule, or another name for the same full moon period; Yule was moved to Christmas and *Þorrablót* stayed where it was (the full moon of the first new moon after the solstice). *Þorri* became the Icelandic month name as it was usually in the Julian (and now Gregorian) month of January, when the full moon of the first new moon after the solstice usually occurred—and still does.

The late fourteenth-century *Flateyjarbók* contains, amongst many other sagas, the only surviving copy of the *Orkneyinga saga* (Saga of the Earls of Orkney) as well as *Hversu Noregr byggðist* (How Norway Was Inhabited). The latter states that Þorri ("Frosty") was a son of Snær ("Snow") who held a midwinter celebration and that from this comes the month name "Þorri." The former states Þorri is the son of Snær and that:

> Þorri var blotmadr mikill. hann hafde blot a hueriu are at midium uetri þat kolludu þeir þorrablot. af þui tok manadrinn hæiti.

> Þorri was a great sacrificer. He held a sacrifice each year at the middle of winter, which they called Þorri's Sacrifice (*Þorrablót*). From this, the month took its name.[22]

Most probably Þorri was originally a presiding deity of the lunar midwinter festival. Like many of the Norse gods, he seems to have been of giant ancestry; his great-great grandfather was Fornjótr ("Old Giant") who appears in a list of names for giants in Snorri's *Skáldskaparmál* and of whom it is said "Forniot's ugly sons first began to send snow."[23]

Like the Æsir themselves in Snorri's *Prose Edda*, Þorri and his family appear to have undergone a process of "euhemerisation," whereby deities are recast as humans. This is an idea from classical antiquity that originated with Euhemerus, a Greek philosopher from the late fourth century BCE, and was taught to Christian clerics in the Middle Ages. Euhemerus wanted to motivate rulers to behave better towards their subjects so he encouraged the notion that the gods were good rulers whom their adoring subjects deified after these rulers died. The idea being that contemporary kings would also be deified after death, if their subjects thought highly enough of them. Mediaeval clerics perhaps wanted to deny that the old gods had ever been divine at all. I expect it

---

22. Old Icelandic text from *Flateyjarbók* (ed. Vigfusson and Unger), I, 219; trans. Moynihan.

23. Snorri, *Edda* (trans. Faulkes), 156 and 93. Faulkes has anglicised the name Fornjótr to Forniot.

was also less of an embarrassing idea that their forebears were mistakenly duped into thinking such ordinary mortals were gods rather than that they had been the outright worshippers of false gods. However, some scholars now suggest that euhemerisation was an idea readily acceptable to Norse people because, as is common the world over, the earliest form of religion was, perhaps alongside animism, ancestor veneration centring around a "cult of the dead."[24]

Many people assume the month called *Þorri* is named after the god Þórr (Thor). Judging from the above, this is clearly not the case. *Þorrablót* is the Old Norse for "Þorri's Sacrifice," whereas "Þórr's Sacrifice" would be *Þórsblót*.

Aside from the information contained in the references above, nothing else is known of Þorri. If one wanted to honour deities at Yule, which would be suitable? Óðinn in his aspect as Jólnir (the "Yule One"),[25] is an obvious choice. However, a case can be made for any deity one chooses; Snorri's *Skáldskaparmál* quotes a line by Eyvindr Skáldaspillir, "Again we have produced Yule-beings' feast [mead of poetry] . . . ," whilst explaining different poetic ways the gods could be described.[26] It would seem all the gods enjoyed Yule as much as those who sacrificed to them! (I have included callings to Þórr and Ullr in the poetry for Yule.)

The Lunisolar Calendar in Anglo-Saxon England

Now to turn to a work of the Venerable Bede, *De temporum ratione* (The Reckoning of Time), written in 725 CE, wherein (cap. XV) we find the author has this to say of the English months:

> In olden time the English people . . . calculated their months according to the course of the Moon. Hence . . . [the months] take their name from the Moon, for the Moon is called *mona*

---

24. For further elucidation of these ideas, see Terry Gunnell's article "How Elvish Were the *Álfar*?" and Laidoner, *Ancestor Worship and the Elite in Late Iron Age Scandinavia*.

25. Jólnir is of Óðinn's many *heiti* (bynames).

26. "*Jólna sumbl, / enn vér gátum.*" Snorri, *Edda: Skáldskaparmál* (ed. Faulkes), I, 85. English from *Edda* (trans. Faulkes), 133.

and the month *monath*.

The first month, which the Latins call January, is *Giuli*, February is called *Solmonath*; March, *Hrethmonath*; April, *Eosturmonath*; May, *Thrimilchi*; June, *Litha*; July, also *Litha*; August, *Weodmonath*; September, *Halegmonath*; October, *Winterfilleth*; November, *Blodmonath*; December, *Giuli*, the same name by which January is called. They begin the year on the 8th kalends of January [25 December], when we celebrate the birth of the Lord. That very night . . . they used to call by the heathen word *Modranecht*, that is, "mother's night" [*sic*],[27] because (we suspect) of the ceremonies they enacted all that night.

Whenever it was a common year, they gave three lunar months to each season. When an embolismic year occurred (that is, one of thirteen lunar months) they assigned the extra month to summer, so that three months together bore the name "*Litha*"; hence they called [the embolismic] year "*Thrilithi*." It had four summer months, with the usual three for the other seasons. But originally, they divided the year as a whole into two seasons, summer and winter, assigning six months in which the days are longer than the nights to summer, and the other six to winter. Hence they called the month in which the winter season began "*Winterfilleth*," a name made up from "winter" and "full Moon," because winter began on the full Moon of that month.

. . . The months of *Giuli* derive their name from the day when the Sun turns back [and begins] to increase, because one of [these months] precedes [this day] and the other follows. . . . *Winterfilleth* can be called by the invented composite name "winter-full."[28]

---

27. The translator's forte is clearly Latin; the Anglo-Saxon word element *Modra-* in *Modranecht* is in the genitive plural, so it should properly be rendered as "Mothers' Night" or "Night of the Mothers."

28. Bede, *The Reckoning of Time* (trans. Wallis), 53–54. Italicization of month names added. The original Latin text of *De temporum ratione* can be found in Bede, *Bedae opera didascalica*, vol. 2.

This tells us that the Anglo-Saxons "of olden times" used the moon to reckon time, employing the use of seven summer months in years when there were thirteen moons. Nowadays, we might see that the Gregorian month of, for example, January has two full moons and call the second one a "blue moon," but in an Anglo-Saxon lunisolar calendar, the "blue moon" would always be inserted between the two moons called "*Litha.*" Why? So that the third new moon before the winter solstice could continue to be Winter-full moon; when that new moon had waxed full, the "lunar new year" was celebrated.

If the year was originally divided into winter and summer, with six moons each (save in an embolismic—thirteen moon—year), winter starts the year, then with two more full moons after the one commencing winter, making three in total, midwinter is reached. When Bede says "The months of *Giuli* derive their name from the day when the Sun turns back [and begins] to increase, because one of [these months] precedes [this day] and the other follows,"[29] he means that the new moon of one of these lunations will precede the solstice and the next new moon will be after the solstice.

Some people maintain that *Giuli* must mean the solstice because of the month names *Ǣrra Gēola* and *Ǣftera Gēola*. But Bede does not use these terms, simply referring to two months both named *Giuli*. The names occur elsewhere in the body of Old English writings that have come down to us. The *Menologium*, a poem on the liturgical year, which prefaced a mid eleventh-century manuscript of the *Anglo-Saxon Chronicle*, mentions *Ianuaris* but not *Ǣftera Gēola*; it has *Ǣrra Iula* at line 221 and at line 108 we find *Ǣrra Līða.*[30] *Ǣrra Gēola* occurs in the *Old English Martyrology*, a collection of hagiographies (lives of saints). In the part for December, it states that *Decembris* is the Latin name for a month called in Old English (or "in our language," as the scribe would probably have put it) *Ǣrra Gēola.*[31] In *Bald's Leechbook*, a ninth-century compendium of Anglo-Saxon herbal medicine, one prescription instructs

29. Bede, *The Reckoning of Time* (trans. Wallis), 54.

30. *Menologium* in Van Kirk Dobbie, ed., *The Anglo-Saxon Minor Poems*, 49–55.

31. Rauer, ed. and trans., *The Old English Martyrology*, 222.

the reader to gather ivy in the month called in Latin *Ianuarius* and in English *Æfterra Gēola* (bk. II, 24).[32]

People tend to see a correlation between *ǣrra* and *æftera* and "before" (or "ere") and "after" in modern English. They argue that Yule was the occasion that had a month before it, named "Before Yule," and a month after it, named "After Yule." However, the Old English words *ǣrra* and *æftera* are not adjectives that describe two nouns; they are comparatives that compare two nouns. (The *-ra* comparative ending has its modern equivalent in "-er," as in heavy/heavier, good/better.) The proper translations of these month names would therefore be "Earlier Yule" and "Later Yule." The Bosworth-Toller *Anglo-Saxon Dictionary* bears this out, giving "hinder, next, second" as the meaning for *æftera*.[33] Again, Yule is not the solstice—the solstice is a marker between two lunations, both called *Gēola* or *Giuli*, just as the two in midsummer are both called *Līða* or *Litha*.

How would people know if, after the winter solstice, instead of the usual twelve there were going to be thirteen full moons before the next winter solstice? Andreas Nordberg has the answer: If there is a new moon within eleven days of the winter solstice, there will be thirteen full moons before the next winter solstice, so people knew the coming year was going to be *Thrilithi* (i.e., having three *Litha* months). Just as such a system ensures that the third new moon before the solstice can continue to commence the Winter-full lunation, so it also means that the second *Giuli* lunation's new moon crescent will never appear in the sky until after the winter solstice.[34]

From this it would seem that *Modranecht* is not Yule, but rather the moon whose new moon appears before the solstice. What, then, are we to make of Bede's remark that the pre-Christian English people "begin the year on the 8th kalends of January [25 December], when we celebrate

32. Cockayne, ed., *Leechdoms, Wortcunning, and Starcraft of Early England*, II, 214. The scribe has written *æftera* with the variant spelling *æfterra*.

33. Bosworth and Toller, *An Anglo-Saxon Dictionary*, under "*æftera*."

34. See Storesund, "Norse Yuletide Sacrifices Had (Almost) Nothing to Do with the Winter Solstice."

the birth of the Lord. That very night . . . they used to call by the heathen word *Modranecht*, that is, 'Mother's [*sic*] night,' because (we suspect) of the ceremonies they enacted all that night"? Let us look first at what "the 8th kalends of January [25 December]" actually means.

Kalends or calends (Latin *kalendae*) is a Roman calendrical term for what was originally the new moon, more specifically the dark of the moon, when no moon was visible at any time of the day or night.[35] The Romans' old calendar was lunar. The strangeness of their reckoning is that the days were counted backwards, so kalends was fourteen nights long, from the dark or new moon, back to the previous full moon. Thus, kalends was the first day (the new moon) of an old Roman month, the day before that was the second day of kalends, and the preceding full moon was the fourteenth kalends day. The *nones* was counted from the first quarter (a waxing "half-moon") back to the new moon and the *ides* was counted backwards from the full moon to the first quarter.

When, by an imperial edict, the Romans adopted a solar calendar invented by Julius Caesar with the help of Greek astronomers and mathematicians—the Julian calendar—they kept the old terms and applied them not to the actual phases of the moon, but to the months of the Julian calendar. Now the kalends of January would be the 1st January, the second kalends of January would be the day before, the 31st December. Working back to the 8th kalends of January would make it the 25th December, and we all know what day that is. The *nones* was the seventh day of any month and the *ides* was the middle of any month (just as the full moon is the middle of any lunation).

Christmas has always been on the 25th December. Why? Because of the Roman festival of Saturnalia. Saturnalia spanned the winter solstice, covering the period of the winter solstice by starting before and finishing after the solstice; it was so thoroughly beloved of the populace that it was extended over time to a week's feasting, drinking, gambling, and general debauchery that lasted from 17th to the 23rd December. In 323

---

35. The word "calendar" derives from Latin *kalendarium*, an account book based on the *kalendae* (the kalends was the traditional day upon which debts were to be paid each month).

CE, Christianity became the official religion of Rome. Saturnalia, far too popular to be banned, continued. The winter solstice then fell on either the 20th or the 21st December, as it does today. Christians would wait a day or two after Saturnalia so that their celebration was distinct from and untainted by the raucous behaviour of the pagan festival. So Christmas did have something to do with a pagan celebration, but a Roman one that did indeed take place over the winter solstice. The Christmas connection though lies not in a usurpation of the pagan celebration, but rather in seeking to distinguish Christmas from Saturnalia, which happened over the solstice period, and so was not displaced by Christmas.

By 725 CE, when Bede wrote *De tempore ratione*, the solstice was on the 17th December. Between 1000 BCE and 2999 CE, the date of the winter solstice varies between the 12th and the 30th December.[36] What was the phase of the moon on 25th December 725 CE, the "very night … they used to call by the heathen word *Modranecht*"?

We must remember that we now use the Gregorian calendar and not the Julian calendar used in Bede's time. I have availed myself of the use of a Julian/Gregorian converter giving the equivalent dates under the two calendrical systems,[37] and the website Moonpage.com, which allows one to calculate the phase of the moon for any Common Era date. The moon phases for the relevant nights of interest in the year 725 CE are as follows:

> 17th Dec. Julian = 21st Dec. Gregorian; Moon waxing, 90% full.
> 20th Dec. Julian = 24th Dec. Gregorian. Moon full.
> 24th Dec. Julian = 28th Dec. Gregorian. Moon waning, 75% full.
> 25th Dec. Julian = 29th Dec. Gregorian. Moon waning, 65% full.

We can see that under the Julian calendar which Bede was using, the solstice on the 17th did not coincide with a full moon, and neither

---

36. https://www.beda.cz/~jirkaj/seasons/seasons.pdf (accessed on 30th April 2021).
37. https://keisan.casio.com/exec/system/1227757509 (accessed on 30th April 2021).

did Christmas Eve or Christmas Day. Furthermore, the solstice did not coincide with Christmas Eve or Christmas Day either. Bede, in this particular instance, appears to be talking out of his venerable posterior. The kindest interpretation one could put on this is that Bede is trying to put across Mothers' Night as a prefiguration of the night Mary gave birth to Jesus. Despite this, he does tell us how the Anglo-Saxon calendar used the solstice as a marker with two lunations called *Giuli*, the first's new moon appearing before the solstice and the second's appearing after. It seems the first Yule month's full moon was Mothers' Night and the second Yule month's full moon was that which was known as plain *jól* in heathen Scandinavia.

Interestingly, Orthodox Christians celebrate Christmas on 25th December—but the 25th of December under the Julian calendar, not the Gregorian which we use today. The Julian calendar had four days' difference in 725; as it continued its inaccuracy, that difference has now grown to thirteen days' difference. Orthodox Christians celebrated Christmas on 7th January 2021 according to the Gregorian calendar. (When Britain adopted the Gregorian calendar in 1752, the difference was eleven days.)

According to the old heathen system of timekeeping, Yule would then be the full moon of the first new moon after the winter solstice. This means that if there is a new moon just after the solstice, the full moon could occur as early as the 5th January; if there was a new moon just before the solstice, then it would be 29.5 days before the first new moon after the solstice and its following full moon would give the 2nd February as the latest "closing date" for a Yule full moon.[38]

Disting

After Yule would come the fifth moon of winter, which many make the case for being the *Disting* moon, associated in Sweden with the *Disting* Fair. This fair, although formally abolished in 1895, has been held

---

38. I was told by a friend who is a Shetlander that in Shetland, there is still recognised an "Auld Yule" (Old Yule). I think this may well represent a folk memory of an older reckoning of time—not necessarily indicative of the date, or even memory, of any lunar festival but just that there once was an older Yule than the current Christmas.

continually from at least the eleventh century down to the present day. This time of *Disting* is associated with the great sacrificial festival held every nine years, known of through the works of Adam of Bremen, Thietmar of Merseburg, and Snorri Sturluson.

I used to think that these great festivals were held at the major and minor lunar standstills. To briefly explain: The sun at the summer solstice dawns in the north-east, rises high in the sky, and sets in the north-west, the longest day. Six solar months later, at the winter solstice, it rises in the south-east and does not get very high in the sky before setting in the south-west, the shortest day. These are the extremes of its rising and setting. What the sun does in a year, the moon does each lunation, every 29.5 days.

Each lunation has its maximum and minimum standstills, just as each year has its winter and summer solstice. The range of these lunar northerly and southerly risings and settings slowly increases and decreases over time. The maximum range is reached at a "major standstill" and the minimum range at a "minor standstill." The range is currently on the increase; it will be 2025 before the moon reaches its peak of northerly rising and setting, its major standstill, when it will rise and set further north than the sun at midsummer. It will also rise and set further south than the sun at midwinter.

This extremity of northerly and southerly rising and setting takes place every 18.6 years. Halfway between them, after 9.3 years, a minor lunar standstill will occur when the monthly range of moonrise and moonset is smallest. Each month the moon will rise and set less to the north than the sun at the summer solstice and also, a fortnight later, less to the south than the sun would be rising and setting at the winter solstice. Its monthly cycle throughout this period will see the moon arc lower in the sky than the sun does at the summer solstice and also each month, a fortnight later, be not as low in the sky as the sun is at the winter solstice.

Neolithic people knew about this nineteen-year cycle. Stonehenge is a 5,000-year-old solar and lunar calendar, or observatory. The stone locations and sightlines not only indicate the summer solstice sunrise and the winter solstice sunset but also the southernmost moonrise, and the northernmost moonset—the latter two alignments will only be observable once every 18.6 years at the moon's major standstill. Because of the particular latitude of Stonehenge, the angle between the point on the horizon where the sun sets on the winter solstice and the point on the horizon where the moon has its most southerly rising is exactly 90°.

I thought that as 2 x 9 = 18, these enneadic festivals would be to mark both the most extreme range of the moon's rising and setting, to witness and celebrate the major lunar standstill, and nine years later, the least extreme range, a minor standstill. I was wrong.

The Swedish archaeo-astronomer Göran Henriksson tells us:

We must note . . . that when the early Swedes said every ninth year this corresponds to every eighth year, as they had no zero and counted the beginning of the first year as year one and reached year nine when only eight years had elapsed.[39]

To put it another way, the ninth year is the first year of the next eight-year cycle. (One cannot help here but to be reminded of the ring Draupnir, referred to in stanza 21 of the Eddic poem *Skírnismál* [The Lay of Skírnir], which drops eight rings of like weight every ninth night.)

Henriksson also states:

It was the German Historian of Astronomy Otto Sigfried Reuter who first realized that *post novem annos* corresponds to every eighth year in our way of counting. Most Swedish scholars, however, continue to believe that it was a true nine-year cycle. In fact, this celebration took place every eighth year according to an eight-year cycle determined by the phases of the moon. The eight-year cycle is the shortest period after which the same lunar phase is repeated approximately on the same date, as eight tropical years = 2921.934 days and 99 synodic months = 2923.528 days.[40]

39. Henriksson, "The Pagan Great Midwinter Sacrifice and the 'Royal' Mounds at Old Uppsala," 15.
40. Henriksson, "The Pagan Great Midwinter Sacrifice," 15.

This eight-year cycle is called the *octaeteris*.

Henriksson talks of eight years being "the shortest period after which the same lunar phase is repeated approximately on the same date,"[41] but another period when the same lunar phase (and its points of rising and setting on the horizon) is repeated on close to the same date of the solar year, is every nineteenth year. The moon will recommence a cycle of rising and setting not only at the same points on the horizon, but also at the same phase. If tonight you were to see an eight-night-old moon rise over your neighbour's chimney pot from your bedroom window, nineteen years later you will see an eight-night-old moon rise over your neighbour's chimney pot from your bedroom window. This nineteen-year cycle is called the Metonic cycle, named after Meton of Athens, a Greek astronomer from the fifth century BCE. The Greeks also referred to it as the *enneakaidekaeteris*, the "cycle of nineteen years."

Earlier I referred to an article by Terry Gunnell, part of which concerns the early mediaeval Swedish law tract, *Upplandslagen*, mentioning a legal gathering, the *disæþing*, and that this was also the occasion of an old festival which Snorri writes is associated with pre-Christian rites. In my section on the *disablót* above, I quoted this passage at length, but to recap: Snorri states that in heathen times in Sweden, the main sacrifices were held at Uppsala in the month of *Gói* (15th February–15th March). By Snorri's time, the now-Christian kings had ceased to reside at Uppsala and the time for the festival had been moved to Candlemas (2nd February).

Snorri is not the only source of information about the festival at Uppsala. An eleventh-century cleric named Adam of Bremen wrote *Descriptio insularum aquilonis* (Description of the Northern Islands [= Scandinavia]), which was part of his history of the church of Hamburg-Bremen (*Gesta Hammaburgensis Ecclesiae pontificium*). It was the Hamburg-Bremen church which controlled the Christian mission to the Nordic lands up until 1105 CE. In the fourth part of his history, Adam gives a description of the rites at Uppsala based upon information from the Danish king Sweyn II Estridsson Ulfsson, who reigned 1047–1074 CE. Gunnell says of Adam's writing:

41. Henriksson, "The Pagan Great Midwinter Sacrifice," 15.

Adam of Bremen's scholium, however, argues that the festival originally took place at the time of the spring equinox . . . this important national festival, while later being dominated by male gods, was originally associated with the *dísir*, whose "name" it retained.[42]

The scholium/scholion (141) that Gunnell is referring to reads:

Novem diebus commessationes et eiusmodi sacrificia celebrantur. Unaquaque die offerunt hominem unum cum ceteris animalibus, ita ut per IX dies LXXII fiant animalia, quae offeruntur. Hoc sacrificium fit circa æquinoctium vernale.

For nine days feastings and that sort of worship are celebrated; on one day they sacrifice one man with other animals, so that through nine days there are seventy-two animals offered. This sacrifice takes place around the spring equinox.[43]

Note it does not state this occurs *on* the spring equinox, but rather "around" it (*circa æquinoctium vernale*).

It seems to me that Snorri was writing about a legal gathering with religious festivities and a market which occurred annually. We know this because it has been held annually down to the present day. It is possible he was referring to the eight-yearly festival which probably would have occurred on the same moon anyway. Either way, Snorri may have been confused here. Nordberg writes:

[I]t is likely that the information given to Snorri did not refer to the Icelandic month, but the Swedish lunar month called *Göje* or *Göja*. This was the third lunar month after the winter solstice in the pre-Christian calendar. The exact date for the *disablot* in

---

42. Gunnell, "The Season of the *Dísir*," 134.

43. Latin text and translation from Tolley, *Shamanism in Norse Myth and Magic*, II (source texts), 104.

Uppsala was probably determined by a full moon—that is, the full moon in the lunar month *Göja*. Expressed in the Gregorian calendar, this could not occur before 5 March, and no later than 3 April.[44]

Adam of Bremen, writing around 1075 CE, is certainly speaking about the eight-yearly festival; the 72 sacrifices indicate a numerical symbolism of 9 x 8. He records in his *Descriptio insularum aquilonis*:

Solet quoque post novem annos communis omnium Sueoniae provintiarum sollempnitas in Ubsola celebrari. Ad quam videlicet sollempnitatem nulli prestatur immunitas. Reges et popoli, omnes et singuli sua dona transmittunt ad Ubsolam, et, quod omni pena crudelis est, illi, qui iam induerunt christianitatem, ab illi se redimunt cerimoniis. Sacrificium itaque tale est: ex omni animante, quod masculinum est, novem capita offeruntur, quorum sanguine deos [tales] placari mos est. Corpora autem suspenduntur in lucum, qui proximus est templo. . . . Ibi etiam canes et equi pendent cum hominibus, quorum corpora mixtim suspensa narravit mihi aliquis christianorum LXXII vidisse.

Also, a celebration, common to all the provinces of Sweden, is customarily held every nine years in Uppsala. No one is exempt from attending this celebration. Kings and people, all and sundry send their gifts to Uppsala, and what is crueller than any punishment is that those who have taken on Christianity buy themselves off from these ceremonies. The sacrifice is of this sort: of every male animal nine individuals are offered, with the blood of which it is the custom to appease such gods. The bodies are hung in the grove, which is very near the temple. . . . There even dogs and horses hang with men, of whose bodies all mixed

---

44. Nordberg, *Jul, disting och förkyrklig tideräkning*, 156. The quote is from the English summary that appears at the end of Nordberg's book.

together one of the Christians told me he had seen seventy-two.[45]

This, along with the above-quoted scholion's statement about it taking place around the spring equinox, would support Nordberg's idea that the old Swedish third lunar month (the sixth and final winter month) was being referred to as the time of year when the eight-yearly sacrifice took place.

A similar rite is recorded in Denmark. Writing in 1012 CE, Thietmar of Merseburg records in his *Chronicon* (I.17):

> *Sed quia ego de hostiis eorundem antiquis mira audivi, haec indiscussa preterire nolo. Est unus in his partibus locus, caput istius regni, Lederun nomine, in pago, qui Selon dicitur, ubi post VIIII annos mense Ianuario, post hoc tempus, quo nos theophaniam Domini celebramus, omnes convenerunt, et ibi diis suimet LXXXX et VIIII homines et totidem equos, cum canibus et gallis pro accipitribus oblatis, immolant . . .*

> But as I have heard remarkable tales of their ancient sacrifices, I do not wish to pass over them without mention. There is one place in these parts, the capital of the kingdom, called Hleiðr (Lejre), in the countryside which is called Selund (Sjælland). In the month of January, after nine years, after the time when we celebrate the Epiphany of the Lord,[46] everyone gathered and they sacrifice to the gods 99 men and as many horses, along with dogs and chickens representing hawks . . .[47]

The 99 sacrifices almost certainly refer to the 99 lunations that take place in eight solar years.

---

45. Latin text and translation from Tolley, *Shamanism in Norse Myth and Magic*, II (source texts), 102–3.

46. Epiphany traditionally falls on 6th January.

47. Latin text and translation from from Tolley, *Shamanism in Norse Myth and Magic*, II (source texts), 101–2.

Henriksson has made a breakthrough in showing that the mounds at Gamla Uppsala are aligned to show a sun setting in the south-west on the 3rd November on its way to its most southerly setting at the winter solstice; three lunations later, the sun sets at the same point on the 8th February as it heads north for its most northerly setting at the summer solstice. Three lunations later, looking along this alignment in the opposite direction, sees the sun rising on the 29th April. If the moon is full on all three of these dates, the sun and moon's cycles coincide and it is the end of one Metonic period and the beginning of another.

Henriksson has also demonstrated that two long rows of postholes discovered in 2013, a short distance south of the later Gamla Uppsala mounds, are orientated to mark the same event. The 600-metre-long row was not orientated towards the setting sun, but towards the rising sun on 8th February. He states that if it was a full moon on that day, the "Great Midwinter Sacrifice" the following year would begin on its earliest possible date, that is to say, the full moon of the earliest possible second new moon after the winter solstice. The 850-metre-long row was aligned to show just that: the following year's rising midwinter full moon. This was the date the Great Midwinter Sacrifice would begin, the start of a new Metonic cycle.[48]

I have searched for historical full moons that fell on 8th February using the moon-phase calculator provided at Moonpage.com and whenever I found one, the following 28th January was also a full moon—not always exactly, but near enough.[49] This is the earliest, according to Henriksson, that a *Disting* moon could possibly take place and indicates the beginning of a new cycle. The February and following January full moons take place every nineteen years or so. It works for February 2020/January 2021; the next time will be February 2039/January 2040. It works for February 852/January 853 CE, the date recorded in the Chronicle of Rimbert for the second visit of Bishop Ansgar to Birka, which states that just before

48. See Henriksson, "The Nordic Calendar and the Great Midwinter Sacrifice at Old Uppsala," 104–9.

49. I should state that I did not check through every decade from the eleventh to twenty-first centuries—that will have to wait for a very rainy day!

his second visit, there had been a great sacrifice. This does argue in favour of Henriksson's assertion that the Great Midwinter Sacrifice was held at *Disting* on the full moon of the second lunation after the winter solstice, not the third as Nordberg believes.

There are several layers of obfuscation that must be taken into account here. The first was the introduction of the erring Julian calendar; then adaptations were made to the way of calculating *Disting* to fit into the Christian liturgical calendar, making Epiphany the "changeover point" rather than the solstice, before moving the *Disting* Fair to Candlemas on 2nd February; and finally, the introduction of the Gregorian calendar.

Nordberg's reckoning would fit in with Bede's description of how the Anglo-Saxons did it. It does make a pleasing symmetry of the year's division into winter and summer moons. It is for this reason that I adopt it. It also fits in with Terry Gunnell's idea that the female ancestral spirits were seen to preside over winter, a time when the female arts of brewing and spinning would have come to the fore. The Norse *dísablót* can be seen to start winter and the Swedish *Disting* to end it. Furthermore, the Anglo-Saxon Mothers' Night is the third full moon of winter; thus, the first, third, and sixth moons all have associations with these beings, albeit associations from different times and places. So, I place the *Disting* moon as the sixth moon, rather than the fifth, of winter. I may well be mistaken.

The event that Henriksson refers to as the Great Midwinter Sacrifice was not something which happened every year. A *Disting* moon does occur every year and Henriksson maintains that when a *Disting* moon also aligned with the mounds and postholes at Gamla Uppsala, it signalled the time when the Great Midwinter Sacrifice would be held. This marked the end of one Metonic cycle and the beginning of another, where a full moon on 8th February is followed by a full moon on the following year's 28th January. These dates, whatever calendar you are using, are marked by alignments—you cannot argue with the mounds and the postholes! However, Henriksson's assertion that the following 28th January is the earliest date at which the second lunation after the solstice could occur is miscalculated; if a new moon fell on the 22nd December, just after the solstice, the earliest date for a full moon of the second lunation after the solstice (which he believes the *Disting* moon to have been) will occur on

2nd February.

What, then, is the significance of a full moon on the 28th January? It would seem that this was simply the time when the cycle was originally observed and confirmed. As I wrote earlier, if you look out of your window tonight and observe the moonrise, one Metonic cycle later it will arise in the same place, at the same time, in the same phase. The Metonic cycle had to commence being observed at some time and within that cycle, any time will do.

A full moon on the 28th January would have waxed from a new moon around the 14th January; a fortnight earlier, there would have been a full moon around the 31st December, which in turn would have waxed from a new moon around the 17th December. That 17th December new moon occurs before the winter solstice; its full moon on 31st December is therefore a "Mothers' Night full moon" (which can occur before or after the winter solstice). The new moon on the 14th January is then the first new moon after the winter solstice. The full moon on the 28th January is therefore a Yule moon: the full moon of the first new moon after the winter solstice (it cannot be the full moon of the second lunation after the solstice). It would not be the earliest possible Yule moon nor the latest possible one, but a Yule moon nonetheless.

To conclude this section, I should mention that the eight- and nineteen-year cycles are what late mediaeval wooden calendar sticks such as the Swedish *runstav*, the Norwegian *primstav*, and the English "clog almanac" predict. These calendar sticks functioned as a perpetual calendar and were certainly still in use in some rural areas of Sweden in 1689, when a farmer from Uppland demonstrated the workings of a *runstav* to the scholar Olaus Rudbeck of Uppsala University.[50]

But how can the observance of an eight-year cycle be resolved with a cycle of nineteen years? A tropical (or solar) year is longer than twelve lunar months: twelve solar months contain a total of 365 days, whereas

---

50. For an interesting connection between the *runstav* calendar and traditional runic poetry, see the discussion of the sixteenth-century "Early Modern Swedish Rune Poem" in Brown and Moynihan, eds., *The Rune Poems*, 49–63.

twelve lunations of 29.5 days make a total of 354 days. Thus, there is usually a difference of eleven days between the two. In some tropical years, however, there will be thirteen lunations, which results in the solar year being shorter than the lunar year: 13 x 29.5 = 383.5 days.

If we take twelve years of twelve lunar months, 12 × 12 = 144 months/lunations, together with seven years of thirteen lunar months ("blue" moons will never be more than 2 years 11 months apart), 7 × 13 = 91 months, and we add the total number of lunar months together, 144 + 91, we get a total of 235 lunar months. If we divide 235 by 12 solar months, we get 19.5, the number of years in the Metonic cycle (integers were not a consideration here). If we divide 235 by 29.5, the length of a lunation, we get 7.966. This shows that a combination of 12 "short" lunar years (with 12 lunations) and 7 "long" years (with 13 lunations) will be equal to 19 solar years. (Neither the Metonic cycle nor the *octaeteris* cycle is exact, but this wouldn't have been an issue to the people at Gamla Uppsala; they would have simply waited for the alignments to mark the known celestial events.)

Here we can clearly see that the moon is not only the measurer of time, but that its cycles were the occasion of the greatest heathen festival that we know of.

I would like to see this heathen festival reinstated. We know that 853 CE was the date of a great sacrifice. In spite of the calculations above, I still do not pretend to fully understand how the observance of an eight-year cycle was resolved in practice with a cycle of nineteen years. Rather than commence a reinstating of the Great Midwinter Sacrifice on some arbitrary date, or on a date based on my admittedly amateur and limited capabilities, I would sooner see unhurried work by specialists— mathematicians, astronomers, and archaeo-astronomers who are interested enough to pick up the cycle correctly.

Sigrblót

As we have seen, *Ynglinga saga* (chap. 8) states: "At the onset of winter, a sacrifice should be made for a good season; and in the middle of winter, a sacrifice for growth of crops; and a third one at summer, which was a sacrifice for victory." I do not think "summer" here means the summer solstice; anyone wanting to go out raiding or campaigning would have been long gone by then and you would surely not hold a festival for victory away from home in hostile country, so far into the "raiding season." Bede's comment, although made of the English, on the months of *Litha* (June and July by his reckoning) is germane to this argument: "*Litha* means 'gentle' or 'navigable,' because in both these months the calm breezes are gentle and they were wont to sail upon the smooth sea."[51]

Folklorist Sandra Billington has shown how early academic assumptions that the midsummer bonfires of mediaeval Europe were pagan survivals do not bear up to closer scrutiny.[52] Again, there is little evidence for a pre-Christian celebration at the summer solstice. Neither Bede nor Snorri mention it.

St. Eligius (588–660 CE), however, probably does mention it. The *Vita S. Eligii* (Life of St. Eligius), gives a typical sermon of the saint— not an actual sermon, but what might be termed a summation of his sermons. Part of it forbids pagan customs: "No Christian on the feast of Saint John or the solemnity of any other saint performs *solestitia* [solstice rites?] or dancing or leaping or diabolical chants." This French bishop did much conversion work in Flanders. The pagan deities he mentions are all Roman—"No Christian should presume to invoke the name of a demon, not Neptune or Orcus or Diana or Minerva or Geniscus."[53] Whether the *solestitia* were something Eligius had observed in his native France or in Flanders, where he converted Frisians and Suevi, is not ascertainable but I would hazard the former.

The Feast of St. John falls on the 24th June whether you are using the Gregorian or Julian calendar; in 660 CE that date in the Gregorian calendar would have been the 27th June. The summer solstice that year was on the 19th June, which would have been 16th June in the Julian calendar. So, the *solestitia* was not an actual solstice celebration, although

51. Bede, *The Reckoning of Time* (trans. Wallis), 54. Italics added.

52. See Billington, "The Midsummer Solstice as It Was, or Was Not, Observed in Pagan Germany, Scandinavia and Anglo-Saxon England."

53. *Vita S. Eligius* (trans. McNamara), Book II.16. It should be noted, however, that Latin accounts often substitute the names of Roman pagan deities for local ones.

the bishop's remark suggests possibly the remnants of one, at least amongst the Gauls.

As was the case with the midwinter festival of Saturnalia, the Romans, who occupied Gaul for hundreds of years, are again the culprits here. Ovid describes the revelry associated with the festival of *Fors Fortuna*, held on the 24th June. Neither Saturn nor Fortuna are solar deities. That Fortuna, *Imperatrix mundi*, should have a festival over the summer solstice was probably the worldly Romans' acknowledgement that the highest, at their peak, could begin to fall. This was happily adopted by the Church as an illustration of how only Christ's ascendency never wanes.

If we were to look at possible midsummer festivities in Iceland, an assumption could easily be made that any summer sacrifices took place at the same time as the Althing, the Icelandic legal assembly. The annual Assembly was established by 930 CE, and from then until 999 CE started on the Thursday of the ninth week after the beginning of summer. Therefore, it was a gathering based on the Icelandic calendar and fell, before the conversion of Iceland to Christianity, around the middle of June. After the conversion, the Althing began on the Thursday of the tenth week of summer—thus, after they became Christian, it shifted nearer to the solstice!

Here they followed the king of Norway, Óláfr Tryggvason, who converted in 994 CE and "got the common people to take up festive drinking at Christmas and Easter, St John's Eve, and . . . Michaelsmass."[54] Yule has already been discussed above, but with regard to the other holidays, Billington notes:

> the pagan beginning of summer was moved to Easter, and Michaelmass is two weeks before the start of the pagan winter. But there was no pagan festival at the summer solstice to be converted. The evidence points to [Óláfr] instituting a new festival on 23/24 June for the people of Norway, in line with the Christianised summer elsewhere in Europe.[55]

54. Quoted in Gunnell, "The Season of the *Dísir*," 123.
55. Billington, "The Midsummer Solstice," 47.

This perhaps explains the reference to midsummer in chapter 65 of the *Óláfs saga Tryggvassonar* (Saga of Óláfr Tryggvasson) where the king agrees to attend a midsummer sacrifice—a *miðsumarsblót*. If this was him trying to introduce his new festival, it clearly intrigued and beguiled the chieftains of Trondheim to accept, leaving the king time to make sure he was not outnumbered the next time.[56] As in Scandinavia, there is no evidence in England of midsummer festivities until after the arrival of Continental influences. If this reference to *miðsumarsblót* were actually the sole surviving reference to pre-Christian religious occasions at midsummer (and I have been unable to find any other), we should, as with the word "midwinter," again be wary of assuming it means the solstice proper. Just as "midwinter" has been shown to be a lunar calendrical occurrence, it would make more sense for the ancient Scandinavians' understanding of *miðsumar* to have also been marked by a full moon. By comparison with midwinter's Yule or *jól*, presumably it would have been the full moon of the first new moon after the summer solstice.

Sandra Billington ends her article by showing how the Roman and subsequent Christian midsummer festivities were occasions for wild dancing, jesting, satire and mockery. "How are the mighty fallen" or how easily might they fall at any time, seems to have been the precept. John the Baptist, himself once thought in his lifetime to be the messiah, but who ended decapitated and dependent on Christ's Salvation, is a Christian exemplar of this, which explains why his feast day was assigned to the 24th June. The raucous festivities were tempered over time; for example, Morris dances came to replace the wilder dancing.

Billington concludes by stating that J. G. Frazer's attribution of midsummer festivities to pre-Christian northern Europe has instigated yet another development of midsummer customs; today, some neopagans who claim to be reinstating pre-Christian Celtic or Germanic festivals include a summer solstice celebration in their ritual calendar. "For scholars, however, concerned with understanding the past, we need to be more clear-sighted than to equate post-Reformation traditions with the

---

56. See Snorri, *Heimskringla* (trans. Hollander), 204–7.

rituals for survival of 2000 B.C.E."[57]

So when would this "third [sacrificial feast] in summer" that is mentioned in *Ynglinga saga* have taken place—could the occasion have been the spring equinox, then moved to Easter after the conversion? Snorri mentions the equinoxes in *Skáldskaparmál*. He states:

> *Frá jafndœgri er haust til þess er sól í eyktarstað. Þá er vetr til jafndœgris. . . . Haustmánuðr heitir inn næsti fyrir vetr, fyrstr í vetri heitir gormánuðr.*

> From the (autumnal) equinox it is autumn until that time when the sun is in *eyktarstaðr*.[58] Then it is winter until the (vernal) equinox. . . . *Haustmánuðr* is the name of last month before winter; the first month in winter is called *Gormánuðr*.[59]

The two months named, *Haustmánuðr* (Autumn-month or Harvest-month) and *Gormánuðr* (Gore-month, i.e., Slaughter-month), occur between mid-September to mid-October, and mid-October to mid-November in the Icelandic calendar. How can "the first [sacrificial feast] in winter" be between mid-October to mid-November when he has already stated that winter occurs between the sun setting in the position of none and the equinox? Because he is using two frames of reference for the year; astronomically, winter is from the solstice to the vernal equinox, but the Icelandic calendar follows an older lore and has winter starting in autumn. There is no evidence here of Icelanders holding celebrations at the solstices and equinoxes. Snorri knew of the equinoxes and if the third sacrifice to celebrate the coming of summer was at the equinox, he would have said so.

To my mind, the third great festival Snorri mentions would have been, like all the others, a lunar one, the first full moon of the six (or

---

57. Billington, "The Midsummer Solstice," 54.

58. The term *eyktarstaðr* refers to the sun's south-west position at mid-afternoon ("none" or in the ninth hour, 3 or 3:30 p.m.) as it sets at the onset of winter in Iceland in mid-October.

59. Snorri, *Edda: Skáldskaparmál* (ed. Faulkes), I, 99; trans. Moynihan.

seven in a "long year") full moons of summer. In the reckoning "of the English people," this would be *Eosturmonath*, "which was once called after a goddess of theirs named Eostre, in whose honour feasts were celebrated in that month."[60] Bede's brief mention of her is the only one there is. *Ostar* is mentioned as a name for the same month in a ninth-century Frankish calendar, but a corresponding deity name of Ostara is not attested.[61]

In Scandinavia, a *sigrblót* or "sacrifice for victory" would surely have involved Óðinn, even if only for a peaceable summer's successful trading in his aspect as Farmatýr, "God of Cargoes" (*Grímnismál*, st. 54).

Excursus: The Bronze Age Cult of the Sun

The worship of the sun in the Bronze Age and in early Iron Age Scandinavia seems evident from the numerous rock carvings there and such wonders as the Trundholm "sun chariot." Interestingly, the Danish archaeologist Klavs Randsborg has suggested that the latter object had a possible function as a calendar—but one of six synodic (lunar) months.[62]

That Bronze Age people would have known of the solstices and equinoxes is beyond dispute. That the winter solstice may have been observed as a way of reconciling the solar and lunar years has already been discussed. Sun worship as such may have died out long before the Viking Age; neither Sól nor Máni, as personifications of the sun and moon, appear to have been the recipients of veneration and certainly have no central role in Norse mythology.

60. Bede, *The Reckoning of Time* (trans. Wallis), 54.

61. The existence of a cognate Continental Germanic goddess named Ostara was proposed by Jacob Grimm in the nineteenth century but has little evidence to support it. For a full study of the questions surrounding Eostre, see the chapter "Eostre: Pan-Germanic Goddess or 'Etymological Fancy'?" in Shaw, *Pagan Goddesses in the Early Germanic World*, 49–72.

62. See Randsborg, "Spirals! Calendars in the Bronze Age in Denmark."

The Poems

1. The First Moon of the Year

Winterfull Moon

The third new moon ere Midwinter Solstice
Has waxed to fullness. Now winter begins.
This light on the land enlivens our minds,
The peak of this power in the pit of our stomachs.

Marking the new year of Máni's seasons;
Ale for Freyr and his elvish wights,
And daughters long dead, *Dísir* kinswomen,
Are festive again in the full moon's light!

An Offering to Freyr

On Winter's Eve, we light this fire,
This growing flame, summer's funeral pyre.
The leaping dancer gives blessings bright
On this stead this holy night.
Leaves fall, long days now are dwindled,
Yet as winter's welcomed, a new year's kindled.

As Álfheim the Gods once gave to Freyr

As a tooth-gift in ancient times,
For the Lord of Light Elves, we light this fire,
Who heated Gerð's heart to summer.

Red deer rut and ripens the sloe berry;
Njörð's one son we name,
Skíðblaðnir's Skipper, Skírnir's friend,
At Gullinbursti's acorn glut!

Peaceful provider, prince of stags,
Bless this beer with luck;
Til árs ok friðar—to fullness and peace,
With plenty a merry twelve month!

This Winter Night, we offer to Freyr,
The stallion, the boar, the stag!
Take well with this ale, this Winterfull moon;
The Bane of Beli we honour.

Álfablót

Bright Elvish Folk of the Otherworld
Living under this land,
Good Hidden Folk hear us; we're haunted by tales
Of your subtle race sublime.

We'd honour you as of old, Elfhame's Dwellers,
Your help and wisdom to have;
Our elder troth to return again:
Fair land, our love, your lore.

Light-elves listen and look upon us,
Incense we offer to you.
We speak with respect, this speech to you,
And libate this barley potion!

Dísablót

The year's cold twilight, counts time in winters,
Each day, each year, with dusk begins;
All grows from the dark. *Dísir* come forth,
Each to their own, ancient kinswomen!
Ghost-girls not forgotten, gather with the darkness,
Your high time is here, this hallowed full moon!
Fine dames on black horses, through Helgrind ride,
Great-grandmothers, from your gravemounds flit,
Bright-browed mothers, from your barrows arise.
Fly to our firesides, to find a welcome,
You ladies who in life spun linen wealth,
Baked the bread and brewed the ale,
Re-forge the bond broken in the past;
Netherworld women, renew the fetters
In the light of this moon, Máni's new year;
Bind bone with bone and be of good cheer.
Let us all drink to Elm, our eldest guest;
The first woman who walked on the world's wide shore,
She's mother to all people, our primal ancestress.
Holy *Dísir* of our families, our distaff sides we honour;
Blood of our blood, about us come,
Whether girls or grandmothers, guardian spirits,
Your descendants drink to their ancestresses' cheer!
And full horns we pour you, of fine mead and beer!

2. The Second Moon of Winter

Now sinks the sun-wheel further south each dusk;
The elf-disk rises at each dawn southward.
Day does dwindle—a dark elf's joy!
Gutters the world's candle. Again, frost falls
From the mane of Night's mount. The moon is vaulting
High up and away, the wolf cannot catch him!
The second moon of winter, sees more darkening,
Night drapes her cloak to cover Day's shoulders,
And draws it tighter, but Day is colder;
Her son seems sickly, and as for Skínfaxi,
His bright mane's duller—frozen dew has more colour.
Outer life's withered, but inner life quivers
When we click off the lights, when we close our eyes,
In the Sleep of the Bear, about us is darkness;
The street lights struggle, and strain to forswear
That only moonlight can help us, only Máni's cold stare.
He shines in the night, and shows us the way
To be brightest in darkness, and blossom in winters.

3. Mothers' Night

The last new moon before midwinter's day
Has waxed to fullness, the waters are rising.
His light on the land enlivens our minds,
The peak of his power in the pit of our stomachs.

The heights he vaults, never higher in the sky,
Winter's middle full moon, is Mothers' Night;
The first, third and sixth, frame the dark door
Of cold wind's drear chorus, it creaks on its hinges,
The "wood-in-the-hole," of winter's blight.
The way in, the way out, but ever shut tight,
Swollen with damp, swiped by rain's spite.
This is the season, for sitting by firelight
And if the house is empty, the hearth still has company;
Our ancient ancestresses, have settled in nicely.
The hearts of all homes, are hallowed places
And haunted in winter, by hidden pale faces,
Women who in life, worked round that glow,
Tending the fire-altar, return in the dark time.
The dead of the night, make draughts that sway curtains,
The swish of a skirt, sweeps on the stair,
The rocking-chair moves, until the rising sun,
They look in on you sleeping, listening to your breathing,
Like Mothers of old, have always done.

(This full moon will sometimes occur before, other times after, the winter
solstice.)

4. Yuletide

Now solstice has brought the sun's growing days
Of lengthening light; if eleven days pass
Without new moon's grace, ere next winter solstice
We'll count twelve moons; a crescent before then
Means thirteen moons and a three-*Litha* summer!

Still high the moon in the holiest of tides;
The stars in the sky—the steersman's guides—
Seem brighter than ever. Reborn, the sun rides.
Yet, a dearth of day and dark is heaven.
The frozen land's beauty is fettered, cold-stricken,
All ice and frost with its eye-catching glisten.
But up we should look—where's Orvandil's Toe?
Þiazi's Eyes aren't in the snow!
A jest, yet no joke is joined to it now:
Mystery you can't master, a masked aloof queen,
Conjured each night yet cannot be seen
In the spray of the stars or the space between.

An Offering to Þórr

Midwinter Nights, we acknowledge Þórr
With offerings says our eldest lore,
And ask for good crops in the coming year;
The gift of Síf's growing hair.

Yet other gifts has Óðinn's son Þórr;
We win a moment's wonder
When lightning strikes, we're struck with awe
When thumps and rolls the thunder.

Shattering giants' skulls, shivering that stone,
Mjöllnir's might's well known,

But the dwarf-forged iron has other powers shown
Than the cracking and crunching of bone;

Bestows bright blessings, restores to life;
It hallows this holy season;
Warding from the blight of winter's strife,
And Yule-Moon's big and bright
With mead makes merry the Heathen!

I offer on this fire, good oaken wood;
Strongest for the strongest god!
And cheering strong liquor for the champion of Ásgarð
I libate on the holy hearth.

An Offering to Ullr

Midwinter's Eve, Ullr's high feast;
We beckon the God of the Bow.
The long northern nights are loved by Þórr's stepson;
The son of Síf wears snow shoes.

Ullr's staff spits forth the striker most silent,
Leaf-bane harms not the yew bough;
Frost glistens Ullr! Your aim is true,
Blend with this drink your blessing.

This drink and fire for the Depth of Winter's God;
We offer to Ullr at Yuletide,
The God of Duels, and good-looking too,
Skis of bone he boasts!

Whether holly was used before the conversion as a decoration for midwinter festivities is not known, but lastly and just for fun I include an "Anacreontic Ode"[1] to the holly below:

Ode to the Holly

Barbed leaves shining, yet so dark,
Each midwinter crown the hearth,
Celebrate the year's cold half.
Matters not the custom's creed,
All to peace on earth accede;
Pagans, heathens, all believe
Over-drinking shows true zeal,
Wine or whisky or real ale,
Bottoms up and make wassail!
"Kiss me quick!" winks Mistletoe,
Make the most of good times' flow
Ere the Reaper lays you low!
When you're gone, Holly will gleam,
Lord of future Yuletide scenes,
Hardwood sprite that's ever green!

---

1. Anacreon was a sixth-century Greek poet. His philosophy was simply that life and life's pleasures, especially those that flowed from the barley and the grape, should be enjoyed to the full—because soon we shall be dead. This has to be the theme of such an ode. Prosodically, the lines should be of seven-syllabled trochaic tetrameter.

5. The Fifth Moon of Winter

The second new moon, since Midwinter's Day.
Has waxed to fullness, the waters are rising.
His light on the land, enlivens our minds,
The peak of his power in the pit of our stomachs.

Each month the moon makes such headway;
North-east rising, and north-west setting,
High in the sky, then hastening southwards,
Difficult to spot in the dawn's pale glow.

The darkest days are done with, over;
To our eyes, the evenings eke out before dusk.
We notice the night is now not so long.
The dark quarter of the year Sköll's Quarry's passed through.

6. The Sixth and Final Moon of Winter

Usually occurring in March, this moon marks the lunar year's end of winter. In seven full moons' time (but see the note below on "long years") will then occur the lunar beginning of winter, which in Germanic tradition commenced the lunar New Year marked by the *álfablót* and the *dísablót*.

Disting Moon

The last moon of winter has waxed to fullness;
Year's dark half's doom? To daylight give way!
Máni's pace doesn't alter, though paler he seems,
When his backdrop's sky blue, and brighter longer.

Washed by the wind, the willow quickens,
Elder leaves sprout, while Alder and Hazel
Have clusters of catkins and clinches of toads
Slowly grapple in the grass. The growing day's time
Soon outstrips the dark. Cold stark winds yet
Are hard on the hare and harass the Rook.
The Wanderer of the Sky watches the world turn,
Hidden or haloed, Hreð's Moon sublime.

The Season of the *Dísir* draws to a close;
Winter's spirit-women
Are stirring themselves, to step out of doors
And wake to the wild once more.

Freyja over the folk, over families their *Dísir*;
Each soul has a following fetch.
All keepers of keys, that close and open
Doors to daylight and darkness.

The hooves of their horses, will be heard again,

In six more sightings of fullness,
They'll unlock the latch, and lift the sneck
And remind you The Mothers know best,
Those girls of the ghostly tide!

If by the time of the full moon the vernal equinox has passed, then the second verse's fifth line should read: "Outstrips the dark. Cold stark winds yet."

In a "long year," where thirteen full moons occur between the last and the next winter solstice (the thirteenth being known nowadays as a "blue moon"), there will be an extra summer month (*Ærra Litha, Litha, Æfterra Litha*) irrespective of the month in the modern calendar in which the two moons occur. This keeps the lunar new year's new moon as being that which is the third new moon before the coming winter solstice and keeps the lunar and solar years synchronised. An easy way to tell if the year will be long, is if a new moon occurs within eleven days of the winter solstice. If it does, the year will be long, so the last verse's second line should then read: "In seven more moons' full measure."

7. The First Moon of Summer

Eostre's Moon

The first moon of summer, the season for travel,
Has waxed to fullness, the waters' high tide.
His light on the land enlivens our minds,
The peak of his power in the pit of our stomachs.

The time of the moon and the tide of the year
Mingle in the magic light.
The Hares' Fair Queen hallows the season,
The daffodils are her daughters.

The lambs now shall live, their leaping brings smiles,
While nests are theeked and renewed.
Bees' beer to the bright moon and spring's beauty I drink;
To the Stag of the Stubble's Lady.

Sigrblót

Father of All, Father of Galdor,
Getter of Gunnlöð's Gift,
Do Huginn and Muninn by your high seat croak?
From that seat you see all worlds!

Maker of Miðgarð, Mímir's Spring's drinker,
Mix your might with this mead;
Sigmund's sword-bringer, Sigurð's horse-giver,
Hallow this horn with your wisdom!

On our ventures all, victory bestow,
So our names are known and remembered!
In each quest we undertake, quicken our luck
For increase in honour well-earned!

For Óðinn, All-Father, this flame ascends;
Glory in fire offerings the gods!
We offer this drink to Óski on high,
The spear-bearing god of speech!

8. The Second Moon of Summer

Second moon of summer, seeming warmer,
You've waxed to fullness, the waters' high tide.
Your light on the land enlivens our minds,
The peak of your power in the pit of our stomachs.

There you are surely! Iðunn's Full Moon;
A round drop of clotted cream.
The light of Night's lantern uplifts eye and mind
While bathing apple blossom in waxing.

The orchards are arrayed with rows of brides,
Standing still they dance.
The moon of romance then makes a shower,
The flower of fruit trees' confetti.

An Offering to Iðunn

On Thrice-milking moon, we make this fire,
To honour the apple queen;
For the gentle goddess, a gift of flame,
For Þiazi's booty, a blazing!

By poetry's potion, the power of your spouse,
Loki's load I call.
As the fruit of the hazel, you flew from Þiazi's,
Fylched by the father of Hel.

Hasten you now here, leave heaven a while,
The girl the gods depend on;
Bear your basket and on Bifröst tread,
So your bubbling joy is about us!

As floods rise from springs, fill this horn,
This ale of the apple with blessing,
So this lake of your luck is lavished in sprinkling
And blessings blossom from drinking!

Take well with this drink, Grim's daughter-in-law,
Who cures Óðinn's kin of old age;
This apple drink we offer to you,
The apple of Bragi's eye!

9. Ere-*Litha* Full Moon

The third moon of summer, like the sun in winter,
Rides near the horizon, reaching no height;
His brief light on the land still enlivens our minds,
The peak of his power in a pale night sky.

Now are full moons near the earth's rim;
The arc of the Sun arches the blue
But low is her brother. In the lithe months of summer,
The Moon and the Sun mirror each other
And keep their distance, though kindred they are.

10. *Litha* Moon (for an Embolismic Year)

The fourth moon of summer, still sinking south-west,
Has waxed to fullness, the waters' high tide.
His light on the land enlivens our minds,
The peak of his power in the pit of our stomachs.

Twelve berserkers sit on the benches
Hearing the chords of the harp.
Twelve are the Gods that gather round the Tree
Well-weighing words of judgement.

Twelve are the halls in the Hooded One's verse;
The harmony of the heavenly garth.
Sunna's pale brother now breaks step with hers,
An off-beat in her order!

To a different drum-beat he dances to his own tune,
A notation of time in nights;
We all moved to this measure when mankind was young,
Tapping our tree-root toes!

11. Later-*Litha* Full Moon

The fourth moon of summer, still sinking south-west,
Has waxed to fullness, the waters' high tide.
Your light on the land enlivens our minds,
The peak of your power in the pit of our stomachs.

Now is your light not needed so much
By farming families—food providers—
Or Edda's kindred, all earthy folk;
A warrior's watch has wide day's help.

A witch must work her ways in brief dark
But Heimdall's highest, hidden in plain sight,
Still feel that force and in fellowship gather;
A moot of like-minds, that remember elsewhere!

In a "three-*Litha*" year, Later-*Litha's* full moon will be the third *Litha*
month's full moon, the fifth moon of the summer half of the year, so first
line would then start: "The fifth moon of summer . . ."

12. Weed Moon

The fifth moon of summer, now setting west-south-west,
Has waxed to fullness, the waters' high tide.
His light on the land enlivens our minds,
The peak of his power in the pit of our stomachs.

On wayside and waste ground, Weed-month is thriving,
On hill and on heath, in hedges, in ditches,
Twisting and trailing, in tangled confusion,
Engorged with growth, grasses and flowers
Wonders to the wise, weeds to the rest,
Lush with folklore, laden with uses,
Or just lovely to look at—a living joy!

Gold-of-pleasure grows in Flax fields;
Scurvygrass ale treats skin and gums;
Milkwort can make a mother's breast flow;
Hogweed and Hemlock, with hollow stems,
Peashooters for the playful, yet one poisons that child;
Woad for a blue, Weld for a yellow,
Cultivated, now outcast, though its colours aren't faded.
The Painted Lady and Peacock's caterpillars
Need the Nettle, yet knees are stung;
Shepherd's purse seed-pods, picked when ripened,
Halve a mother's heart in two;
Aaron's rod was Fairy's wand, an older truer name;
Scentless Midsummerwort soon sends ghosts away;
Enchanter's nightshade, a charm against elves;
The scent of Honeysuckle on a summer's evening!
Placed on a pillow—pleasing dreams follow!
The Hawk moth homes in on Hedge bindweed,
Flowers open nightlong—only if there's a moon—
Unlike shuttered others, it shines back white!

Over hedgerow and harvest, a higher moon climbs.
While leaf and man take life from the sun,
For plants and people a power is drawn
From the well in the sky, that waters our roots,
That feeds our souls, that fades with the dawn.

In a "three-*Litha*" year, this moon will be sixth moon of summer. The first line would then commence: "The sixth moon of summer . . ."

13. Holy Moon

Matching the sun's path, mingling tracks,
The sixth moon of summer, sets in the west,
Now waxed to fullness, the waters are rising.
His light on the land enlivens our minds,
The peak of his power in the pit of our stomachs.

Holy-Moon are you called, hallowing the season;
The culling of corn takes place.
Blades are busy, biting through crops;
Sif's Hall is a harvest field.

For thousands of years, the threshing's gone on,
Bending the back with its burden,
But for many thousands more than man can recall,
A work-free harvest is happening.

It fed us once, before farming's lordship,
Still feeds the feathered and furred;
Oak-corns rain down, dive in free-fall,
Boars' snouts are snuffling them out.

The berries are ripening, bright reds and purples
And the heart of the Hazel on her sleeve!
Holy-Moon gleam on that grove of Crab-apples;
We'd munch immortals' food!

Many the moons that made you the final,
The last of the lunar year.
How can I be sure? A secret few know;
To make match the moon and sun's years.

Your new moon crescent was counted the fourth
Ere next Solstice Eve.

The third new moon meets the winter;
When full, to the *Dísir* we drink.

Then Elves are honoured with ale of the best.
But now, this night is yours;
Your brimful moon as bright as any
Reckoning the rounds of time.

This will be the seventh moon of summer in a "long year." The second line would then begin: "The seventh moon of summer . . ."

BIBLIOGRAPHY

Bede. *Bedae opera didascalica*, vol. 2. Edited by C. W. Jones. Turnhout: Brepols, 1977.

————. *The Reckoning of Time*. Translated by Faith Wallis. Liverpool: Liverpool University Press, 2004.

Beowulf. Translated by Michael Swanton. Manchester: Manchester University Press, 1997.

Billington, Sandra. "The Midsummer Solstice as It Was, or Was Not, Observed in Pagan Germany, Scandinavia and Anglo-Saxon England." *Folklore* 119.1 (April 2008): 41–57.

Bosworth, Joseph, and T. Northcote Toller. *An Anglo-Saxon Dictionary*. Oxford: Oxford University Press, 1980.

Brown, P. D., and Michael Moynihan, eds. *The Rune Poems: A Reawakened Tradition*. North Augusta, S.C.: Gilded Books, 2022.

Cleasby, Richard, and Gudbrand Vigfusson. *An Icelandic-English Dictionary*. Second edition, with a supplement by W. A. Craigie. Oxford: Clarendon, 2003 [1957].

Cockayne, Thomas Oswald, ed. *Leechdoms, Wortcunning, and Starcraft of Early England*. 3 vols. London: Longman, Green, Longman, Roberts, and Green, 1864–1866.

[*Flateyjarbók*]. *Flateyjarbok: En samling af Norske konge-sagær med indskudte mindre fortællinger om begivernheder i og udenfore Norge samt annaler*. Edited by Guðbrandur Vigfusson and C. R. Unger. 3 vols. Christiania [Oslo]: Malling, 1860–1868.

Gísla saga Súrssonar. Edited by Finnur Jónsson. Halle: Niemeyer, 1903.

Gunnell, Terry. "How Elvish Were the *Álfar?*" In *Constructing Nations, Reconstructing Myth: Essays in Honour of T. A. Shippey*, edited by Andrew Wawn, with Graham Johnson and John Walter. Turnhout: Brepols, 2007. Pp. 111–30.

———. "The Season of the *Dísir*: The Winter Nights, and the *Dísablót* in Early Scandinavian Belief." *Cosmos* 16.2 (June 2000): 117–49.

Henriksson, Göran. "The Nordic Calendar and the Great Midwinter Sacrifice at Old Uppsala." In *The Materiality of the Sky*, edited by Fabio Silva, Kim Malville, Tore Lomsdalen, and Frank Ventura. Ceredigion, Wales: Sophia Centre Press, 2016. Pp. 99–110.

———. "The Pagan Great Midwinter Sacrifice and the 'Royal' Mounds at Old Uppsala." In *Calendars, Symbols, and Orientations— Legacies of Astronomy in Culture: Proceedings of the 9th annual meeting of the European Society for Astronomy in Culture (SEAC), held at the Old Observatory in Stockholm, 27–30 August, 2001*, edited by Mary Blomberg, Peter E. Blomberg, and Göran Henriksson. Uppsala: Uppsala University, 2003. Pp. 15–27.

Heselton, Philip. *In Search of the New Forest Coven.* [Nottingham, U.K.]: Fenix Flames, 2020.

Hutton, Ronald. *The Triumph of the Moon.* Oxford: Oxford University Press, 1999.

Klaeber, Friedrich, ed. *Beowulf.* Fourth revised and expanded edition edited by R. D. Fulk, Robert E. Bjork, and John D. Niles. Toronto: University of Toronto Press, 2008.

Laidoner, Triin. *Ancestor Worship and the Elite in Late Iron Age Scandinavia: A Grave Matter.* London and New York: Routledge, 2020.

McKinnell, John. *Meeting the Other in Norse Myth and Legend.* Cambridge: Brewer, 2005.

Nordberg, Andreas. *Jul, disting och förkyrklig tideräkning: Kalendrar och kalendariska riter i det förkristna Norden.* Uppsala: Kungl. Gustav Adolfs Akademien för svensk folkkultur, 2006.

Randsborg, Klavs. "Spirals! Calendars in the Bronze Age in Denmark." *Adoranten* (2009): 1–11.

Rauer, Christine, ed. and trans. *The Old English Martyrology: Edition, Translation and Commentary.* Woodbridge: Brewer, 2013.

Shaw, Philip A. *Pagan Goddesses in the Early Germanic World: Eostre, Hreda and the Cult of Matrons.* London: Bristol Classical Press, 2011.

Simek, Rudolf. *Dictionary of Northern Mythology.* Translated by Angela Hall. Woodbridge, UK: Brewer, 1993.

————. *Religion und Mythologie der Germanen.* Darmstadt: Theiss, 2003.

Snorri Sturluson. *Edda.* Translated by Anthony Faulkes. London: Dent, 1987.

————. *Edda: Prologue and* Gylfaginning. Edited by Anthony Faulkes. London: Viking Society for Northern Research, 1988.

————. *Edda: Skáldskaparmál.* Edited by Anthony Faulkes. 2 vols. London: Viking Society for Northern Research, 1998.

————. *Heimskringla: Nóregs konunga sǫgur.* Edited by Finnur Jónsson. 4 vols. Copenhagen: Møller, 1893–1901.

————. *Heimskringla.* Translated by Lee M. Hollander. Austin:

University of Texas Press, 1999.

Storesund, Eirik. "Norse Yuletide Sacrifices Had (Almost) Nothing to Do with the Winter Solstice." https://www.brutenorse.com/blog/2017/12/norse-yuletide-sacrifices-had-almost.html (accessed 27 April 2021).

Tacitus. *The Agricola and the Germania*. Translated by H. Mattingly and S. A. Handford. London: Penguin, 1987.

———. *The Germania of Tacitus*. Edited by Henry Furneaux. Oxford: Clarendon, 1894.

Thorsson, Edred [Stephen E. Flowers]. *History of the Rune-Gild: The Reawakening of the Gild, 1980–2018*. North Augusta, S.C.: Gilded Books, 2019.

Tolley, Clive. *Shamanism in Norse Myth and Magic*. 2 vols. Helsinki: Academia Scientiarum Fennica, 2009.

Van Kirk Dobbie, Elliott, ed. *The Anglo-Saxon Minor Poems*. New York: Columbia University Press, 1942.

[*Vita S. Eligii*]. *The Life of St. Eligius, 588–660*. Translated and annotated by Jo Ann McNamara. Fordham University Medieval Sourcebook. https://sourcebooks.fordham.edu/basis/eligius.asp (accessed 10 July 2022).

Whaley, Diana, ed. *Poetry from the Kings' Sagas 1: From Mythical Times to c. 1035*. Turnhout: Brepols, 2013.

Other titles available from Arcana Europa and Gilded Books:

The Rune Poems: A Reawakened Tradition

Edited by P. D. Brown and Michael Moynihan

ISBN 979-8410339742, 249 pages, paperback, $24.00

The word *rune* literally means a "secret" or "mystery." But how does one begin to unravel the mystery of the runes? One good place to start is the traditional rune poems, which are provided here in concise yet elegant—not to mention heavily annotated—translations: the *Old English Rune Poem*, the *Old Norwegian Rune Rhyme*, and the *Old Icelandic Rune Poem*, as well as the lesser known *Abecedarium Nordmannicum* and the *Early Modern Swedish Rune Poem*. These oddly compelling verses are a storehouse of gnomic wisdom and early Germanic cultural lore, and their purpose was surely more than just an aid for committing the runic alphabets to memory—as many modern scholars would have us believe. In his introduction, English poet P.D. Brown suggests that the poems were instead tools "to make the mind more generally agile, more adept at making connections, thinking 'laterally' and more imaginatively" about what the runes in fact *are*.

This is also the purpose of the twenty modern rune poems included in this volume, which have been composed over the past four decades by members of the Rune-Gild, an international order that includes scholars and storytellers, poets and artists, musicians and magicians. Like the rune poems of old, these modern compositions encapsulate years—and in many cases, decades—of close study and intense reflection. Traditional and innovative at the same time, and expressed in a myriad of styles, these new poems demonstrate that the runes are much more than an object of idle antiquarian curiosity. They are living mysteries whose depths—like the roots of the World Tree Yggdrasil—will never be fully fathomed.

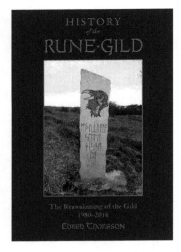

History of the Rune-Gild: The Reawakening of the Gild 1980–2018

Edred Thorsson

ISBN 978-0-999724-4-5, 270 pages, paperback, $24.00

Edred Thorsson (Stephen Flowers) is the world's foremost expert on esoteric runology. He founded the Rune-Gild in 1979 as an initiatory organization tasked with the creation of Rune-Masters who could carry this knowledge forward to new generations. Unlike other occult or esoteric organizations, however, the Gild's focus is not only on techniques of magic and self-transformation. The Gild strives to provide its Learners, Fellows, and Masters with a rigorous scholarly perspective for situating these techniques within the broader context of Germanic and Indo-European history and tradition, which is the underlying foundation of our culture.

In this fascinating and informative volume, Thorsson describes his childhood as a "monster kid" in the late 1950s and early 1960s, and documents the first stirrings of *Rûna*—or "the Mystery"—in his life. He describes his formative (and often humorous) experiences with various occult organizations and the strange and eccentric personalities whom they attract. He chronicles his distinguished academic career and his relationship with scholarly mentors like Prof. Dr. Edgar Polomé and Prof. Dr. Klaus Düwel. He provides the background for his connections to the world of occult publishing and his involvement with neopagan (or heathen) organizations like the Asatru Free Assembly and the Ring of Troth. Thorsson also speaks candidly of his more controversial associations, such as with Dr. Michael Aquino's Temple of Set, or with the sexual subculture of sadomasochism—affiliations that have given rise to considerable misunderstandings and moralizing gossip. Throughout these pages, Thorsson approaches his own life and work with surprising honesty, both as to his successes and—in some cases—his failures. But even when the path has been fraught with difficulties and unforeseeable obstacles, Thorsson has relied on the hidden hand of the "Old Man" (Odin or Woden) to guide his life's mission of (re-)establishing a traditional Rune-Gild in North America and Europe.

Made in United States
Orlando, FL
18 August 2023

36176455R10050